The Aquarian Sun Sign Guides

ARIES

Bernard Fitzwalter has been interested in astrology since he was about six, when he played King Herod's astrologer in his primary school nativity play. For the past six years he has been teaching astrology for the Marylebone-Paddington Institute, and for seven years he has had a regular column in OVER 21 magazine. In 1984 he appeared in the first series of Anglia Television's *Zodiac Game*, which prompted the *Daily Mirror* to say that he was 'enough to give astrology a good name'.

AQUARIAN SUN SIGN GUIDES

ARIES

21 MARCH - 19 APRIL

Bernard Fitzwalter

Cover illustration by Steinar Lund
Cover typography by Steven Lee

THE AQUARIAN PRESS
Wellingborough, Northamptonshire

First published 1987

© BERNARD FITZWALTER 1987

British Library Cataloguing in Publication Data

Fitzwalter, Bernard
Aries.—(The Aquarian sun sign guides)
1. Zodiac
I. Title
133.5'2   BF1726

ISBN 0-85030-579-9

*The Aquarian Press is part of the
Thorsons Publishing Group*

Printed and bound in Great Britain

Contents

PART 4: ARIES TRIVIA

Introduction

This book has been written to help you find out a little about astrology and a lot about yourself. It explains, for the first time, the motives and aims that guide your actions and make you do things the way you do; what it does not do is give you a list of 'typical Aries' things to see if you recognize any of them. You are not likely to be typical anything: you are unique. What you *do* have in common with others who have birthdays at about the same time as you is a way of using your energy, a way of thinking, a set of motives and beliefs which seem to make sense to you, and which other people, those of the other eleven signs, obviously do not have. This book shows you those motives and beliefs, and shows you how they fit in with those of the other eleven signs. The zodiac is like a jigsaw: all the pieces have to be there for the whole picture to emerge.

This book also sets out to answer some very simple questions which are often asked but seldom answered. Questions like 'Why does the zodiac have twelve signs?' and 'What does being an Aries actually mean?' as well as 'Why are Arians supposed to be temperamental? Why can't they be placid instead? and why don't all the people of the same star sign look the same?'

The reason that these questions are seldom answered is because all too many astrologers don't know the rudiments of astrological theory, and what they do know they don't tell, because they think it is too difficult for the man in the street to understand. This is obvious nonsense: astrology was devised for and by people who did not normally read or write as much as we do, nor did they all have PhDs or the equivalent. The man in the street is quite capable of understanding anything provided that it is shown simply and clearly, from first principles upwards, and provided he has sufficient interest. Buying this book is evidence enough of your interest, and I hope that the explanations are simple enough and clear enough for you. If they are not, it is my fault, and not that of astrology.

How to Use this Book

The book is in four parts. It is best to read them in sequence, but if you have neither time nor patience, then they each work individually. Part 2 does not assume that you have read Part 1, though it helps. Part 3 makes a lot more sense if you have already read Parts 1 and 2, but it isn't mandatory. Part 4, although just as firmly based on astrological principles as the other three, is deliberately intended as light relief.

The first part of the book deals with the theory behind the zodiac; it sets out the principles of astrology and enables you to see why Aries is assigned the qualities it has, how the ruling planet system works, and what all the other signs are like in terms of motivation, so you can compare them to your own. There is a short and effective method given for assessing the aims and motives of other people. When you read Part 3 you will need to know a bit about the other signs, as you will be finding out that you have more to you than just the Aries part you knew about.

The second part describes the essential Aries. It shows you how there are different sorts of Arians according to where your birthday falls in the month, and shows how Arian energy is used differently in the Arian as a child, adult, and parent.

Since you spend the greatest part of your life in dealing with other individuals, the way Aries deals with relationships is treated in some detail. This is the largest section of the book.

The third part shows you a different kind of zodiac, and

enables you to go into your own life in much greater detail. It isn't complicated, but you do need to think. It crosses the border between the kind of astrology you get in the magazines, and the sort of thing a real astrologer does. There's no reason why you can't do it yourself because, after all, you know yourself best.

The fourth part shows you the surface of being an Arian, and how that zodiacal energy comes out in your clothes, your home, even your favourite food. The final item of this part actually explains the mechanics of being lucky, which you probably thought was impossible.

I hope that when you finish reading you will have a clearer view of yourself, and maybe like yourself a little more. Don't put the book away and forget about it; read it again in a few months' time—you will be surprised at what new thoughts about yourself it prompts you to form!

Note

Throughout this book, the pronouns 'he', 'him', and 'his' have been used to describe both male and female. Everything which applies to a male Arian applies to a female Arian as well. There are two reasons why I have not bothered to make the distinction: firstly, to avoid long-windedness; secondly, because astrologically there is no need. It is not possible to tell from a horoscope whether the person to whom it relates is male or female, because to astrology they are both living individuals full of potential.

BERNARD FITZWALTER

Part 1

How the Zodiac Works

1. The Meaning of the Zodiac

Two Times Two is Four; Four Times Three is Twelve

It is no accident that there are twelve signs in the zodiac, although there are a great many people who reckon themselves to be well versed in astrology who do not know the reasons why, and cannot remember ever having given thought to the principles behind the circle of twelve.

The theory is quite simple, and once you are familiar with it, it will enable you to see the motivation behind all the other signs as well as your own. What's more, you only have to learn nine words to do it. That's quite some trick— being able to understand what anybody else you will ever meet is trying to do, with nine words.

It works like this.

The zodiac is divided into twelve signs, as you know. Each of the twelve represents a stage in the life cycle of solar energy as it is embodied in the life of mankind here on our planet. There are tides in this energy; sometimes it flows one way, sometimes another, like the tides of the ocean. Sometimes it is held static, in the form of an object, and sometimes it is released when that object is broken down after a period of time. The twelve signs show all these processes, both physical and spiritual, in their interwoven pattern.

Six signs are used to show the flowing tide, so to speak, and six for the ebbing tide. Aries, Gemini, Leo, Libra, Sagittarius, and Aquarius are the 'flowing' group, and the others form the second group. You will notice at once that the signs alternate, one with the other, around the zodiac, so that the movement is maintained, and there is never a concentration of one sort of energy in one place. People whose Sun sign is in the first group tend to radiate their energies outwards from themselves. They are the ones who like to make the first move, like to be the ones to take command of a situation, like to put something of themselves into whatever they are doing. They don't feel right standing on the sidelines; they are the original have-a-go types. Energy comes out of them and is radiated towards other people, in the same way as the Sun's energy is radiated out to the rest of the solar system.

The people in the other signs are the opposite to that, as you would expect. They collect all the energy from the first group, keeping it for themselves and making sure none is wasted. They absorb things from a situation or from a personal contact, rather than contributing to it. They prefer to watch and learn rather than make the first move. They correspond to the Moon, which collects and reflects the energy of the Sun. One group puts energy out, one group takes it back in. The sum total of energy in the universe remains constant, and the two halves of the zodiac gently move to and fro with the tide of the energies.

This energy applies both to the real and concrete world of objects, as well as to the intangible world of thoughts inside our heads.

A distinction has to be made, then, between the real world and the intangible world. If this is done, we have four kinds of energy: outgoing and collecting, physical and mental. These four kinds of energy have been recognized for a long time, and were given names to describe the way they work more than two thousand years ago. These are the elements. All the energy in the cosmos can be described in the terms of these four: Fire, Earth, Air, Water.

Fire is used to describe that outgoing energy which applies to the real and physical world. There are three signs given to it: Aries, Leo, and Sagittarius. People with the Sun in any of these signs find themselves with the energy to get things going. They are at their best when making a personal contribution to a situation, and they expect to see some tangible results for their efforts. They are sensitive to the emotional content of anything, but that is not their prime concern, and so they tend to let it look after itself while they busy themselves with the actual matter in hand. Wherever you meet Fire energy in action, it will be shown as an individual whose personal warmth and enthusiasm are having a direct effect on his surroundings.

Earth is used to describe the real and physical world where the energies are being collected and stored, sometimes in the form of material or wealth. The three signs given to the element are Taurus, Virgo, and Capricorn. Where Fire energy in people makes them want to move things, Earth energy makes them want to hold things and stop them moving. The idea of touching and holding, and so that of possession, is important to these people, and you can usually see it at work in the way they behave towards their own possessions. The idea is to keep things stable, and to hold energy stored for some future time when it will be released. Earth Sun people work to ensure that wherever they are is secure and unlikely to change; if possible they would like the strength and wealth of their situation to increase, and will work towards that goal. Wherever you meet Earth energy in action, there will be more work being done than idle chat, and there will be a resistance to any kind of new idea. There will be money being made, and accumulated. The idea of putting down roots and bearing fruit may be a useful one to keep in mind when trying to understand the way this energy functions.

Air is used to describe outgoing mental energies; put more simply, this is communication. Here the ideas are formed in the mind of the individual, and put out in the hope that they can influence and meet the ideas of another individual; this is communication, in an abstract sense. Gemini, Libra, and Aquarius are all Air signs, and people with the Sun in those signs are very much concerned with communicating their energies to others. Whether anything gets done as a result of all the conversation is not actually important; if there is to be a concrete result, then that is the province of Fire or Earth energies. Here the emphasis is on shaping the concept, not the reality. There is an affinity with Fire energies, because both of them are outgoing, but other than that they do not cross over into each other's territory. Wherever you meet Air energy in action, there is a lot of talk, and new ideas are thrown up constantly, but there is no real or tangible result, no real product, and no emotional involvement; were there to be emotional content, the energies would be watery ones.

Water is the collection of mental energies. It is the response to communication or action. It absorbs and dissolves everything else, and puts nothing out. In a word, it is simply feelings. Everything emotional is watery by element, because it is a response to an outside stimulus, and is often not communicated. It is not, at least not in its pure sense, active or initiatory, and it does not bring anything into being unless transformed into energy of a different type, such as Fire. Cancer, Scorpio and Pisces are the Water signs, and natives of those signs are often moody, withdrawn, and uncommunicative. Their energy collects the energy of others, and keeps their mental responses to external events stored. They are not being sad for any particular reason; it is simply the way that energy works. It is quite obvious that they are not showing an outgoing energy, but neither have they anything tangible to show for their efforts, like the money and property which seem to accumulate around Earth people. Water people simply absorb, keep to themselves, and do not communicate. To the onlooker, this appears unexciting, but there again the onlooker is biased: Fire and Air energies only appreciate outgoing energy forms, Earth energies recognize material rather than mental energies, and other Water energies are staying private and self-contained!

We now recognize four kinds of energy. Each of these comes in three distinct phases; if one zodiac sign is chosen to represent each of these phases within an element, there would be twelve different kinds of energy, and that would define the zodiac of twelve, with each one showing a distinct and different phase of the same endless flow of energy.

The first phase, not surprisingly, is a phase of definition, where the energies take that form for the first time, and where they are at their purest; they are not modified by time or circumstance, and what they aim to do is to start things in their own terms. These four most powerful signs (one for each element, remember) are called cardinal signs: Aries, Cancer, Libra, Capricorn. When the Sun enters any of these signs, the seasons change; the first day of the Sun's journey through Aries is the first day of spring, and the Spring equinox; Libra marks the Autumnal equinox, while Cancer and Capricorn mark Mid-summer's Day and the shortest day respectively.

The second phase is where the energy is mature, and spreads itself a little; it is secure in its place, and the situation is well established, so there is a sort of thickening and settling of the energy flow. Here it is at its most immobile, even Air. The idea is one of maintenance and sustenance, keeping things going and keeping them strong. This stage is represented by Taurus, Leo, Scorpio, and Aquarius, and they are called, unsurprisingly, fixed signs. These four signs, and their symbols, are often taken to represent the four winds and the four directions North, South, East and West. Their symbols (with an eagle instead of a scorpion for Scorpio) turn up all over Europe as tokens for the evangelists Luke, Mark, John and Matthew (in that order).

The final phase is one of dissolution and change, as the energy finds itself applied to various purposes, and in doing so is changed into other forms. There is an emphasis on being used for the good, but being used up nonetheless. The final four signs are Gemini, Virgo, Sagittarius, and Pisces; in each of them the energies of their element are given back out for general use and benefit from where they had been maintained in the fixed phase. It is this idea of being used and changed which leads to this phase being called mutable.

Three phases of energy, then; one to form, one to grow strong and mature, and one to be used, and to become, at the end, something else. Like the waxing, full, and waning phases of the Moon.

The diagram on page 16 shows the twelve signs arranged in

their sequence round the zodiac. Notice how cleverly the cycle and phases interweave:

(a) Outgoing and collecting energies alternate, with no two the same next to each other;

(b) Physical ebb and flow are followed by mental ebb and flow alternately in pairs round the circle, meaning that the elements follow in sequence round the circle three times;

(c) Cardinal, fixed, and mutable qualities follow in sequence round the circle four times, and yet

(d) No two elements or qualities the same are next to each other, even though their sequences are not broken.

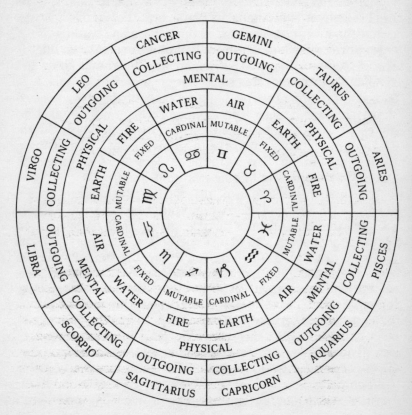

The interweaving is perfect. The zodiac shows all forms of energy, physical and mental, outgoing or incoming, waxing or waning, harmoniously forming a perfectly balanced unity when all the components are taken together. Humanity, as a whole, contains all the possibilities; each individual is a component necessary to the whole.

All this can be a bit long-winded when what you want is some way of holding all that information for instant recall and use, which is where the nine words come in.

If a single word is used for the kind of energy flow, and another two for the element and quality, then they can be used to form a sentence which will describe the way the energy is being used.

As a suggestion (use other words if they are more meaningful to you), try 'outgoing' and 'collecting' for the energy flows.

Next, for the elements:

Fire :	activity	(Aries, Leo, Sagittarius)
Earth :	material	(Taurus, Virgo, Capricorn)
Air :	communication	(Gemini, Libra, Aquarius)
Water :	feelings	(Cancer, Scorpio, Pisces)

And for the qualities:

Cardinal :	defining	(Aries, Cancer, Libra, Capricorn)
Fixed :	maintaining	(Taurus, Leo, Scorpio, Aquarius)
Mutable :	using	(Gemini, Virgo, Sagittarius, Pisces)

Now in answer to the question 'What is a Gemini doing?' and answer can be formed as 'He's outgoing, and he's using communication', which neatly encapsulates the motivation of the sign. All that you need to know about the guiding principles of a Gemini individual, no matter who he is, is in that sentence. He will never deviate from that purpose, and you can adapt your own actions to partner or oppose his intention as you please.

A Scorpio? He's collecting, and he's maintaining his feelings. An Arian? He's outgoing, and he's defining activity. And so on.

Those nine words, or some similar ones which you like better, can be used to form effective and useful phrases which describe the motivation of everybody you will ever meet. How different people show it is their business, but their motivation and purpose is clear if you know their birthday.

Remember, too, that this motivation works at all levels, from the immediate to the eternal. The way a Taurean conducts himself in today's problems is a miniature of the way he is trying to achieve his medium-term ambitions over the next two or three years. It is also a miniature of his whole existence: when, as an old man, he looks back to see what he tried to do and what he achieved, both the efforts and the achievement, whatever it is, can be described in the same phrase with the same three words.

2. The Planets and the Horseshoe

You will have heard, or read, about the planets in an astrological context. You may have a horoscope in a magazine which says that Mars is here or Jupiter is there, and that as a consequence this or that is likely to happen to you. Two questions immediately spring to mind: What do the planets signify? How does that affect an individual?

The theory is straightforward again, and not as complex as that of the zodiac signs in the previous chapter. Remember that the basic theory of astrology is that since the universe and mankind are part of the same Creation, they both move in a similar fashion, so Man's movements mirror those of the heavens. So far, so good. If you look at the sky, night after night, or indeed day after day, it looks pretty much the same; the stars don't move much in relationship to each other, at least not enough to notice. What do move, though, are the Sun and Moon, and five other points of light—the planets. It must therefore follow that if these are the things which move, they must be the things which can be related to the movements of Man. Perhaps, the theory goes, they have areas of the sky in which they feel more at home, where the energy that they represent is stronger; there might be other places where they are uncomfortable and weak, corresponding to the times in your life when you just can't win no matter what you do. The planets would then behave like ludo counters, moving round the heavens trying to get back to a home of their own colour, and then starting a new game.

The scheme sounds plausible, makes a sort of common sense, and is endearingly human; all hallmarks of astrological thought, which unlike scientific thought has to relate everything to the human experience. And so it is: the planets are given values to show the universal energy in different forms, and given signs of the zodiac as homes. Therefore your Sun sign also has a planet to look after it, and the nature of that planet will show itself strongly in your character.

The planets used are the Sun and Moon, which aren't really planets at all, one being a satellite and the other a star, and then Mercury, Venus, Mars, Jupiter, and Saturn. This was enough until the eighteenth century, when Uranus was discovered, followed in the subsequent two hundred years by Neptune and Pluto. Some modern astrologers put the three new planets into horoscopes, but it really isn't necessary, and may not be such a good idea anyway. There are three good reasons for this:

(a) The modern planets break up the symmetry of the original system, which was perfectly harmonious;

(b) The old system is still good enough to describe everything that can happen in a human life, and the modern planets have little to add;

(c) Astrology is about the relationship between the sky and a human being. An ordinary human being cannot see the outer planets on his own; he needs a telescope. We should leave out of the system such things as are of an extra-human scale or magnitude: they do not apply to an ordinary human. If we put in things which are beyond ordinary human capabilities, we cannot relate them to the human experience, and we are wasting our time.

In the diagram on page 21 the zodiac is presented in its usual form, but it has also been split into two from the start of Leo to the start of Aquarius. The right hand half is called the solar half, and the other one is the lunar half. The Sun is assigned to Leo because in the Northern hemisphere, where astrology started, August is when you feel the influence of the Sun most, especially in the Eastern Mediterranean, where the Greeks and the other early Western civilizations were busy putting the framework of astrology together in the second millennium BC. The Sun is important because it gives light. The Moon gives light too; it is reflected sunlight, but it is enough to see by, and this is enough to give the Sun and Moon the title of 'the Lights' in astrology. The Moon is assigned to Cancer, so that the two of them can balance and complement each other. From there, moving away from the Lights around the circle on both sides, the signs have the planets assigned to them starting with the fastest mover, Mercury, and continuing in decreasing order of speed. Saturn is the slowest mover of all, and the two signs opposite to

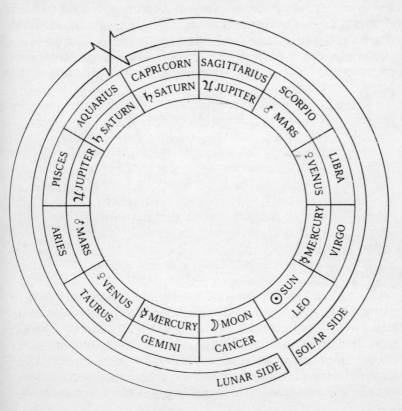

the Lights are both governed by that planet. The reasons for this apparent assymmetry will be explained in a little while. This arrangement is, of course, the horseshoe of the title to this chapter.

The Sun and Moon work in a similar fashion to the outgoing and collecting energies we noted earlier with the twelve signs. The Sun is radiant above all else; energy comes outwards from it, warming and energizing all those around it. Leo people, whose sign is the Sun's, work like this by being at the centre of a group of people and acting as inspiration and encouragement to them all. The Moon reflects the Sun's light, and energies of a lunar kind are directed inwards towards the core of the person. The two energies are necessarily linked; lunar people would starve without the solar folks' warmth, but the solar types need someone to radiate to or their purpose is unfulfilled.

The planets on each side of the horseshoe display their own energies in a solar or lunar way depending on which side of the pattern they are on.

Mercury and Venus form a pair, representing complementary but opposite ideas, which should be familiar by now. Mercury represents difference, and Venus stands for similarity.

Wherever anything new forms that is distinguishable from the background, then Mercury is there making it what it is, highlighting what makes it different. Anything separate is Mercurial, and words, since they are separate and can be strung together into millions of different combinations, are Mercurial too. Mercury is not a long-term influence; it notes things as being different for an instant, and then they become part of the establishment, and something else is new elsewhere. Because 'new' is an instantaneous state—that is, something can only be new once, and for a moment—Mercury is not associated with anything lasting, and its rapid motion as a planet leads to its being associated with the idea of speed. Virgo, Mercury's solar sign, is concerned with the changing of the shape of things ('collecting, using material' in our keyword system), while Gemini, the lunar sign, is concerned with reading and writing, and getting new ideas ('outgoing, using communication').

Venus does the reverse; it looks for that which is similar, finding points of contact to make relationships between common interests and energies. It likes to preserve the harmonies of life, and resents anything which might interrupt them. Love and affection are naturally Venusian, but so is music and all of the Arts, for the harmonies they contain. Expressed in a solar way, Venus is Libra, the maker of relationships; its lunar face is Taurus, emphasizing food and furnishings as things which give pleasure to the individual.

The next pair are Mars and Jupiter. Mars applies force from the outside to impose structure on a disordered universe, while Jupiter expands forcibly from the inside to give growth and wealth, inviting everyone else to join in.

Mars is pure force, energy in a straight line with a direction to go in. Anger and passion are both Martian, and so is lust, because they are all examples of great energy directed towards a given end. Note that Martian force is not necessarily strength, wealth, or know-how, just pure energy, which often boils over and needs controlling. Mars is the power in an athlete, and in an assassin too. It is also the power in a lover, because the urge to create is also the urge to pro-create, and if that energy fulfils its purpose then that creation takes place. Scorpio is its solar side, the power to control and create; in lunar form it is shown by Aries, as energy enjoyed for its own sake by its owner, with no purpose except to express it.

Jupiter is the spirit of expansion from within; not only does it oppose Mars' force from outside, it opposes Mars' physicality with its own mental emphasis. Jupiter develops the mind, then. As it does so, it develops all natural talents of an academic nature, and encourages movement, enquiry and travel to broaden experience and knowledge. The Solar expression of this is Sagittarius, where the centaur symbol is both a wise teacher and a free-roaming wild horse at the same time. Jupiter in a lunar sense is Pisces, where the imagination is developed to a greater extent than anywhere else, but used to provide an internal dream world for the owner's pleasure. Great sensitivity here, but the lunar energies are not of the sort to be expressed; rather other energies are *im*pressed on the Piscean mind.

Saturn is the last of the five planets. He stands alone, and if it is necessary to consider him as paired with anything it is with the Lights as an entity together. The Lights are at the centre of the system; Saturn is at its edge. They are the originators of the energies of the zodiac, and he is the terminator. Everything to do with limits and ends is his. He represents Time, and lots of it, in contrast to Mercury, which represented the instant. He represents the sum total of all things, and the great structures and frameworks of long-term endeavour. In solar form he is Capricorn, the representative of hard work, all hierarchies, and all rulers; in lunar form he is Aquarius, showing the horizontal structure of groups of people within society at different levels. Here he denies the activity of Mars, because society is too big for one person to change against the collective will, and he contains the expansion of Jupiter within himself. Venus and Mercury can neither relate to it nor make it change, because it is always the same, in the end.

The planets show important principles in action, the same as the zodiac does. You have probably noticed that the horseshoe of the planets and the ring of the zodiac say the same thing in a different way, and that is true about most things in astrology. It may be that the two systems interrelate and overlap because they are from the same source: after all, $3+2+2=7$, which is the planet's total, and $3\times2\times2=12$, which is the signs'. How you assign the elements and qualities, pairs of planets and lights is for you to decide. The joy of astrology, like all magic, is that it has you at the centre, and is made to fit its user's requirements. Now you know the principles, you can use it as you please, and as it seems relevant to you.

Part 2

Yourself—and Others

3. The Essential Aries

All the energy in the zodiac is solar, but that solar energy takes many forms. It is moderated and distributed through the planetary energies until it finally shows in you, the individual. As an Aries, the prime planetary energy is that of Mars; you will be motivated by, and behave in the manner of, the energies of Mars. To remind yourself of what that means, read the section on the Moon on page 23. As a sign of the zodiac, Aries is a Cardinal Fire sign. Remind yourself what that means by reading page 15. Now we have to see how those essential principles work when expressed through a person and his motivation.

What it Means to be an Aries

You know what it is to be an Aries, because you are one; but you probably don't know what it is that makes an Aries the way he is, because you cannot stand outside yourself. You would have to be each of the other eleven signs in turn to understand the nature of the energy that motivates you. This essential energy is in every Arian, but it shows itself to different extents and in different ways. Because it is in every single Arian, it is universal rather than specific, and universal ideas tend to come in language which sounds a little on the woolly side. You will think that it isn't really about what makes you who you are, because you don't feel like that every day—or at least you think you don't. In fact, you feel like that all the time, but you don't notice it any more than you notice your eyes focusing, yet they do it all the time, and you see things the way you do because of it.

The first thing to note is that the zodiac is a circle, not a line with a beginning and an end. If it were a line, then Aries would be at the beginning of it, but that would be to miss the point; if the zodiac is a circle, then Aries is a stage in an endlessly repeating cycle, and we will get a much better idea of what it is if we look to see where it came from, and where it is going.

The sign before Aries is Pisces. Pisces represents the dissolution of all that is definite, the breaking down into component parts, and further down into elements. All things are possible in Pisces at a universal level, but nothing has any form. Nothing exists, or does not exist; nothing has direction, shape, or connection with anything else. From this primeval soup of endless possibility, energies meet and coalesce; possibility becomes probability; direction and purpose are drawn together. Finally, they become a single point of focused energy—the beginning of separate existence. This energy must start the new cycle of things. It must be strong enough to be the initiator of other processes which will take up where it leaves off. It must be sure of its own purpose, for it has to make new things from nothing, using only itself. It is sure, like nothing else is, of its own existence, and confident of its own strength; it can say 'I am myself' when everything else in the universe is unformed and without direction. This is the spirit of Aries, the beginning of the cycle, the spark of creation.

Biologically it corresponds to a spermatozoon and the moment of conception; a package of possibilities made definite at a single point, a living thing whose sole purpose is to make a beginning.

An Arian does not feel particularly spiritual; other signs have time for reflection, but the Arian does not. You know simply that you are, and that you are individual. You need to do what you feel you would like to do; this is not through some wayward urge to be different, although later social contact and conditioning may make it so, nor is it from a desire to be seen to be doing something others could not, and thus acquire glamour and notoriety, though it may be a convenient face to put on things, if people seem to view it so. The desire is much too simple for that; it is simply a desire to exist on your own terms. You do not need to create or maintain anything, because that would put your energies into something which is not yourself, and suggest that there are more important things to you than your own existence. You do not need to break things down and re-create them to be the way you want them to be, because that involves spending some of your existence ensuring the non-existence of other things. You have no need for that; you are not threatened by any other thing that is, because you know that you are yourself, untouched by other forces.

Completion and maintenance are not part of the Arian vocabulary; seeing a project grow to completion and fullness of form does not concern you, any more than keeping it going and continuing its purpose. Beginning is what you are best at. You have almost no concept of time; you may grow one to enable you to understand others, but the pure energy of Aries lives in an eternal present, where tomorrow is a long time away, next year almost impossible to believe, and yesterday doesn't matter any more.

This sense of immediacy extends to your own experience, which must be actual for you to appreciate it. In other words, you have to do it for yourself. Reading the instruction book is not something you do; you switch on and push all the buttons to see what happens for yourself. This tendency to rush in and touch, to make things happen with your own hands, leads to a lot of accidents, especially on those days when the energy flow isn't quite as strong as you remember it being. Blades and other sharp things seem to have an affinity for you, and you discover how sharp they are time and time again, confident either in your ability to avoid accident or in your desire to see just how sharp they are. You are usually mistaken, and it is something you learn again and again.

Arian energy flows through the whole of the body, and

therefore you think in terms of its use all the time. Where the Gemini, for example, thinks nothing of his body, but lives in his mind, you are the other way round; you use your body for everything, and gain satisfaction from doing so. Sports and any kind of exertion are a pleasure to you. The idea of laziness, as in a disinclination to do anything physically, is alien to you. You may well be disinclined to do something because you are not interested in it, but not because you don't like exerting yourself. Arians get dubbed 'pioneers of the zodiac', a title which suggests a sort of hardy, self-denying loner driven on to new horizons by a desire to be first. All this is true to some extent, but it is misleading. You are not driven by anything to do anything; you do what appeals to you, and you use all your energy in a direct and physical way to achieve that, without thought for what happens later. A good example is a footballer heading the ball; all his thoughts go into using his head to direct the ball. He does not care, as he leaps to make the shot, where he lands after his head has hit the ball; he will only become aware of a need to land somewhere after his head has hit the ball. That's how Arians work.

Aries corresponds to the head of the body. Arians have big heads, sometimes, and strong skulls with noticeable eyebrows. The head leads the rest of the body, and Aries leads the rest of the zodiac. The head is where most of your sense organs are located, and Arians like to feel things directly. Arians also get headaches and similar problems when they are under stress, but in matters of health there are other considerations, and some of them will be examined later.

Sexually, an Arian again expresses his energy physically. A sexual relationship for an Arian is based on physical sensation more than anything else. Sexual satisfaction does not come to an Arian through togetherness or mutual affection, nor through intellectual rapport; it is found entirely in the physical sensations of using the body to express desire, and enjoying the sensations felt by the body in return for that energy output. Pure, and simple; uncomplicated, unaffected by other considerations, it is simply a person whose body is his most important possession using it to communicate desire to another body.

To sum up, if you want a single adjective to remind you how an Arian has to do things, it is 'headlong'. Head first, at full speed, completely absorbed in the experience of the action, and without a thought for his own safety or the consequences—that's how Arians do things, like the Ram which represents the sign.

Early, Middle or Late? The Decanates

Each of the zodiac signs is divided into degrees, like an arc of any other circle. Since a circle has 360 degrees, then each sign must be 30 degrees, since there are twelve signs. Each of the signs is further split into sections of ten degrees, called decanates. There are three decanates in each sign, and the one that your birthday falls in will tell you a little more about how that Arian energy actually works in you as an individual.

First decanate (21–30 March)
This is the purest form of Aries. There is a double helping of Martian energy here, expressed as an irrepressible form of outward-looking, enthusiastic optimism. You will have a special zest for life; you will feel that you are in some way special and different from everybody else, because you have that spark of independence which knows that nothing is ever going to go wrong for you. What you don't do is share yourself in any way; you are too involved in the action itself to think of companionship when you really think about it. Thinking about it doesn't happen very often either; such is the speed and the passion of your way through life, that you seem never to think things through; you may say that you don't need to, and you would be right to some extent, but there is an appreciation which comes from examining things after the event to see what they can teach you, and this you will never see. Nor do you bother to see how much, or how well, you can do things; to you, the action itself is enough, and you trust your own abilities; there may be other abilities which you will never discover, or improvements on your

known talents which you will never make. That's double Mars for you—it never looks back, and it never has time.

Second decanate (31 March–9 April)

Here Aries is moderated a little and the Sun helps Mars to turn some of its boundless energy into warmth rather than movement. You will be keen to develop your personality and your talents, where the earlier decanate does not. You will still be dashing and full of life, but somehow there is a warmth to you which others find inspiring, and you enjoy being a leader to some extent, whereas the earlier decanate is very much a loner in essence. You will be keen to do as much as you can with yourself, and wherever you think you have some ability you will take care to develop it, thinking as you do that it is better to be able to do things yourself than to have others do them for you, and better yet to do them *well* yourself. Much more of your energy will be put into showing what you can do; your achievements are somehow more visible than those of other Arians. People like being near you; your flair and enthusiasm seem to transfer to everyone.

Third decanate (10–19 April)

Aries' Martian energy works through Jupiter in the final section of the sign, bringing thoughtfulness to bear on the immense power of Mars, and spreading it out a little rather than concentrating it. There is also a change of emphasis from the strictly personal to the more general. The Arian here feels that he is indeed uniquely gifted with a capacity for effective action, but that he ought to use this carefully and to the best effect. He thinks before he acts, and he uses some of his direct energy in his thinking processes, giving a clear and decisive mind not always found in the other Arians. He also thinks that he must consider the impact of his actions on others, and if possible act to their benefit. Sometimes this gets stuck in his mind and a preoccupation with some consideration or other arises—a sort of 'one-track mind' caused by the Arian simplicity of approach coupled with instant decisions and the usual Arian inability to wait for things to happen—but at least the intention is good. This is the only Arian to consider using his energy for anything other than a personal, and short-term, goal; the way he uses his energy contrasts sharply with the first decanate, where the energy almost uses the person.

Three Phases of Life: Aries as Child, Adult, Parent

The Aries child
Arians seem to be the most lively children, and thoroughly enjoy their childhood. The problems come later, when they show a marked reluctance to stop being children and adopt adult behaviour patterns.

As children, they are bouncy and energetic, full of energy and into anything and everything. They adore being outside where they can run, climb, swim, play games, and generally tire themselves out; the next day they are ready to do it all again, as though each day was the first time they had ever experienced such delights. To a certain extent it is, because they are slow to build a sense of time or accumulated experience. The girls are just as active as the boys, and favour the same kind of activities. When they are put into a classroom, they work hard and well as long as their attention is kept, but that is not often for long. Because they get bored so easily, and have no sense of anything being necessary as well as no sense of time, they do not concentrate for as long as some oher children. As a result, their schoolwork can be a bit haphazard, both in the quality of presentation, and in the depth of understanding behind it. They are at their best where they are allowed or encouraged to show their own thoughts—English essays will be fast-moving and amusing, though they could end abruptly, showing that something else has disturbed the creative flow and diverted interest elsewhere! They need to learn to consider other people than themselves, which they find difficult, and some degree of tidiness and organization for later life, though any parent who hopes to get an Arian child to develop much of this is fighting a losing battle. It is not possible, and not desirable, to suppress the

energy of the Arian child, but it is possible to channel it
constructively.

The Arian adult
The Arian adult retains most of the child's characteristics; this is
in direct contrast to the Capricorn adult, who seems to be born as
an adult, and seems never to display any childish qualities, even
as an infant!

The desire to suit himself is still there, as is the lack of
organization. Although he is decisive, the decisions are usually
not based on careful consideration, but on the first solution that
comes into his head, according to the theory that any action is
better than no action. It never occurs to him that other people
might have better solutions, or cheaper ones. It also never
occurs to him that other people might not be in agreement with
the solution adopted, so he does not bother to ask them. He is
completely without regard for risk or danger, and this can lead to
accidents. An injured adult Arian is sometimes an amusing sight:
like a child who has fallen and grazed his knee, he is in complete
amazement that such a thing could ever have happened to him,
and tearfully blames Fate for this wicked and unmerited mishap
which has completely and irretrievably shattered his faith in the
world. For five minutes, that is, until something else has taken
his mind and interest away from it all.

Arian adults need to find a physical outlet for their energies,
and most of them play some sort of sport, the more demanding
the better. They are not particularly good team athletes, because
their energy centres around themselves; they are much more
suited to individual competition.

Having unstructured thought processes which change every
few minutes makes Arians original and opinionated, though not
particularly profound thinkers. Often their capacity for saying
what they think at the moment that it occurs to them makes for
some biting humour, and they tend to develop a sharp sense of
humour which enjoys satire and cynical one-liners. They do not
enjoy sophisticated humour or verbal wit; if it is funny
immediately and without having to think about it, then they

laugh. That said, they like puzzles, but only if they can solve them without too much difficulty; like children, they appreciate finding something for themselves, but they won't try very hard to get it.

The Arian parent

Arian parents are both very pushy, because the Martian energy pushes through them into the children; just how they are pushy depends on the sex of the parent.

An Arian father wants the child to be like him, to be an extension of the things that he has chosen to do. He also wants the child to be Arian because that's all he himself knows how to be, and he can't imagine life any other way. If the child is Arian, or at least has the Sun in a Fire sign, then he might fit in well with his father's wishes, but if he is of a different, gentler, nature, such as a Piscean or a Virgoan, then there will be problems because the Arian father will not be able to understand his way of thinking. It is, of course, a mistake for the Arian father to insist that the child do Arian things in an Arian way. Considerable care and tolerance is needed on both sides to make this relationship free of stresses.

An Arian mother does not want her child to be like her, but she does want her child to be as effective and successful as she is; she wants her child to be number one and at the front, in a very Arian way, at whatever the child does. Children are an extension of herself, to an Arian mother; if they are hurt, she is hurt. At school, if the child is unfairly treated or injured in any way, the Arian mother is there to complain to the headmaster, as though she herself had been hurt. Whatever talents her child shows, which may not of course be Arian ones, will receive full support from the Arian mother, so that every talent can be fully and energetically expressed. The only problems are that she is sometimes interested only to develop talents in the child that she herself has, or wishes she had (her child may not choose to do anything with these abilities), and that she sometimes feels that only she can direct and aid the child's progress, becoming too dominant for the child's good. When the child does grow up and away, she is left feeling cheated of something she regarded as hers for all time, which, of course, was not true.

4. Aries Relationships

How Zodiacal Relationships Work

You might think that relationships between two people, described in terms of their zodiac signs, might come in 144 varieties; that is, twelve possible partners for each of the twelve signs. The whole business is a lot simpler than that. There are only seven varieties of relationship, although each of those has two people in it, of course, and the role you play depends on which end of the relationship you are at.

You may well have read before about how you are supposed to be suited to one particular sign or another. The truth is usually different. Arians are supposed to get on with Leos and Sagittarians, and indeed they do, for the most part, but it is no use reading that if you have always found yourself attracted to Scorpios, is it? There has to be a reason why you keep finding Scorpios attractive, and it is not always to do with your Sun sign; other factors in your horoscope will have a lot to do with it. The reason you prefer people of certain signs as friends or partners is because the relationship of your sign to theirs produces the sort of qualities you are looking for, the sort of behaviour you find satisfactory. When you have identified which of the seven types of basic relationship it is, you can see which signs will produce that along with your own, and then read the motivation behind it explained later on in more detail in

'The Aries Approach to Relationships' and the individual compatibility sections.

Look at the diagram on page 16. All you have to do is see how far away from you round the zodiacal circle your partner's Sun sign is. If they are Virgo, they are five signs in front of you. You are also, of course, five signs behind them, which is also important, as you will see in a little while. If they are Capricorn, they are three signs behind you, and you are three signs in front of them. There are seven possibilities: you can be anything up to six signs apart, or you can both be of the same sign.

Here are the patterns of behaviour for the seven relationship types.

Same sign

Somebody who is of the same sign as you acts in the same way that you do, and is trying to achieve the same result for himself. If your goals permit two winners, this is fine, but if only one of you can be on top, you will argue. No matter how temperamental, stubborn, devious, or critical you can be, they can be just the same, and it may not be possible for you to take the same kind of punishment you hand out to others. In addition, they will display every quality which really annoys you about yourself, so that you are constantly reminded of it in yourself as well as in them. Essentially, you are fighting for the same space, and the amount of tolerance you have is the determining factor in the survival of this relationship.

One sign apart

Someone one sign forward from you acts as an environment for you to grow in. In time, you will take on those qualities yourself. When you have new ideas, they can often provide the encouragement to put them into practice, and seem to have all your requirements easily available. Often, it is this feeling that they already know all the pitfalls that you are struggling over which can be annoying; they always seem to be one step ahead of you, and can seemingly do without effort all the things which you have to sweat to achieve. If the relationship works well, they are helpful to you, but there can be bitterness and jealousy if it doesn't.

Someone one sign back from you can act as a retreat from the pressures of the world. They seem to understand your particular needs for rest and recovery, whatever they may be, and can usually provide them. They can hold and understand your innermost secrets and fears; indeed, their mind works best with the things you fear most, and the fact that they can handle these so easily is a great help to you. If the relationship is going through a bad patch, their role as controller of your fears gets worrying, and you will feel unnerved in their presence, as though they were in control of you. When things are good, you feel secure with them behind you.

Two signs apart
Someone two signs forward from you acts like a brother or sister. They are great friends, and you feel equals in each other's company; there is no hint of the parent-child or master-servant relationship. They encourage you to talk, even if you are reticent in most other company; the most frequently heard description of these relationships is 'We make each other laugh'. Such a partner can always help you put into words the things that you want to say, and is there to help you say them. This is the relationship that teenagers enjoy with their 'best friend'. There is love, but it does not usually take sexual form, because both partners know that it would spoil the relationship by adding an element of unnecessary depth and weight.

Someone two signs behind you is a good friend and companion, but not as intimate as somebody two signs forward. They are the sort of people you love to meet socially; they are reliable and honest, but not so close that things become suffocatingly intense. They stop you getting too serious about life, and turn your thoughts outwards instead of inwards, involving you with other people. They stop you from being too selfish, and help you give the best of yourself to others. This relationship, then, has a cool end and a warm end; the leading sign feels much closer to his partner than the trailing sign does, but they are both satisfied by the relationship. They particularly value its chatty quality, the fact that it works even better when in a group, and its tone of affection and endearment rather than passion and obsession.

Three signs apart
Someone three signs in front of you represents a challenge of some kind or another. The energies of the pair of you can never run parallel, and so must meet at some time or another. Not head on, but across each other, and out of this you can both make something strong and well established which will serve the two of you as a firm base for the future. You will be surprised to find how fiercely this person will fight on your behalf, or for your protection; you may not think you need it, and you will be surprised that anybody would think of doing it, but it is so nonetheless.

Someone three signs behind you is also a challenge, and for the same reasons as stated above; from this end of the relationship, though, they will help you achieve the very best you are capable of in a material sense. They will see to it that you receive all the credit that is due to you for your efforts, and that everyone thinks well of you. Your reputation is their business, and they will do things with it that you could never manage yourself. It's like having your own P.R. team. This relationship works hard, gets results, and makes sure the world knows it. It also looks after itself, but it needs a lot of effort putting in.

Four signs apart
Someone four signs forward from you is the expression of yourself. All the things you wanted to be, however daring, witty, sexy, or whatever, they already are, and you can watch them doing it. They can also help you to be these things. They do things which you think are risky, and seem to get away with them. There are things you aim towards, sometimes a way of life that you would like to have, which these people seem to be able to live all the time; it doesn't seem to worry them that things might go wrong. There are lots of things in their life which frighten you, which you would lie awake at nights worrying

about, which they accept with a child's trust, and which never go wrong for them. You wish you could be like that.

Someone four signs behind you is an inspiration to you. All the things you wish you knew, they know already. They seem so wise and experienced, and you feel such an amateur; luckily, they are kind and caring teachers. They are convincing, too. When they speak, you listen and believe. It's nice to know there's somebody there with all the answers. This extraordinary relationship often functions as a mutual admiration society, with each end wishing it could be more like the other; unfortunately, it is far less productive than the three-sign separation, and much of its promise remains unfulfilled. Laziness is one of the inherent qualities of a four-sign separation; all its energies are fulfilled, and it rarely looks outside itself for something to act upon. Perhaps this is just as well for the rest of us.

Five signs apart

Someone five signs ahead of you is your technique. You know what you want to do; this person knows how to do it. He can find ways and means for you to do what you want to be involved in, and he can watch you while you learn and correct your mistakes. They know the right way to go about things, and have the clarity of thought and analytical approach necessary if you are to get things clear in your mind before you get started

Someone five signs behind you is your resource. Whenever you run out of impetus or energy, they step forward and support you. When you're broke, they lend you money, and seldom want it returned. When you need a steadying hand because you think you've over-reached yourself, they provide it. All this they do because they know that it's in their best interest as well as yours, to help you do things, and to provide the material for you to work with. You can always rely on them for help, and it's nice to know they will always be there. They cannot use all their talent on their own; they need you to show them how it should be done. Between you, you will use all that you both have to offer effectively and fully, but it is a relationship of cooperation and giving; not all the zodiac signs can make it work well enough.

Six signs apart

Someone six signs apart from you, either forwards or backwards, is both opponent and partner at the same time. You are both essentially concerned with the same area of life, and have the same priorities. Yet you both approach your common interests from opposite directions, and hope to use them in opposite ways. Where one is private, the other is public, and where one is self-centred, the other shares himself cheerfully. The failings in your own make-up are complemented by the strengths in the other; it is as if, between you, you make one whole person with a complete set of talents and capabilities. The problem with this partnership is that your complementary talents focus the pair of you on a single area of life, and this makes for not only a narrow outlook, but also a lack of flexibility in your response to changes. If the two of you are seeing everything in terms of career, or property, or personal freedom, or whatever, then you will have no way to deal effectively with a situation which cannot be dealt with in those terms. Life becomes like a seesaw; it alternates which end it has up or down, and can sometimes stay in balance; but it cannot swing round to face another way, and it is fixed to the ground so that it does not move.

These are the only combinations available, and all partnerships between two people can be described as a version of one of the seven types. It must be remembered, though, that some of the roles engendered by these dispositions of sign to sign are almost impossible to fulfil for some of the signs, because their essential energies, and the directions they are forced to take by the planets behind them, drive them in ways which make it too difficult. To form a relationship based on sharing and acceptance is one thing: to do it when you are governed by a planet like Mars is somethings else. Even when the relationship can form, the sort of approach produced by, say, Jupiter, is a very different thing from that produced by Venus.

The next thing you must consider, then, is how you, as an Arian, attempt relationships as a whole, and what you try to find in them. Then you must lay the qualities and outlook of each of the twelve signs over the roles they must play in the seven relationship types, and see whether the pair of you manage to make the best of that relationship, or not.

The seven relationship types are common to all the signs, relating to all the other signs. You can use your understanding of them to analyse and understand the relationship between any pair of people that you know, whether or not they are Arian; but to see how the characters fit into the framework in more detail, you will need to look at the individual compatibilities, of which just the Arian ones are given in this book.

The Arian Approach to Relationships

An Aries is wholly motivated by his need to experience things first-hand as a result of his own actions and decisions. He is entirely self-motivating, self-sustaining, and self-centred. Most people read the word 'self-centred' as if it meant 'selfish', but that is not the case here. 'Self-centred' here means centred on the self; not centred on any ambition, possession, political persuasion, religion, friend, relative, or circumstance, just on the self.

It will seem obvious to you, as an Arian reading this, that your self matters most, and it is very difficult for you to imagine anybody thinking any other way; but the fact is, that only Arians, and people of other signs born with Mars, Aries' planet, in important places in the sky, do think this way, and that the vast majority of humanity does not.

When you enter a relationship, therefore, you are seeking to express yourself physically to the other person, and experience their response to you. You want to experience the excitement of being in love, or of having a new partner, and you want them to excite you with their response, but you do not necessarily consider them as people in themselves, and never think that you might have to put aside your own requirements to serve their needs. That's just not how you think, and it is wrong for people to criticize you for not holding an attitude which is completely alien to you.

When you do fall in love, when you have decided that projecting all your energy at an individual is so rewarding that you can think of nothing that you would rather do, you do it with all the power that your planet, Mars, gives you—and that is a great deal. Your partner is likely, whatever their sign, to be surprised at the passion you generate. Not just sexual energy, but the intensity of the emotions you can unleash. Have you ever been surprised at how strong a baby is? When they want something, they go for it with all the strength they have, whereas adults, conditioned by their ideas of polite behaviour, don't do anything with that kind of total dedication; as a result, adults find the strength, intensity, and single-minded dedication of infants surprising. Arians work in exactly the same way as babies. The energy generated by a full-grown adult, when applied with the single-minded dedication of a young child, is a little frightening; other people experience an Arian in love with them as being like this. This can be a bit much to take all at once, especially if the object of your affections is unused to such passionate displays. There is a lot of the child in your character, and you are likely to try to win people over in ways which would win *you* over. You know how quickly your mood changes, and how delighted you are with anything new and personal to you; you love getting presents, and so you give them too, in the hope that if you like them, others will. This usually works, but again it can be a bit overwhelming to be given lots of surprise gifts if you are uncertain about the relationship anyway.

Mars makes you sexually very powerful and expressive, and this has rarely caused an Arian any difficulty in relationships, provided that this power stays within the relationship and doesn't extend to other partners at the same time. Arians tend to be one-at-a time folk, though; they focus on one person, and pursue that one person alone. Aries doesn't take the same delight in variety as, say, Sagittarius.

As a friend, it is the immediacy and open enthusiasm you generate that is attractive to other people, and you will find yourself attracted to anybody who displays those same qualities to you. No matter what their sign, if they have confidence in their actions, and they appear to be assertive and active, you will find yourself admiring them, and eventually meeting them (an Arian meets people, of course, by walking over to them and introducing himself; he never waits to be introduced). The only other sort of person you find attractive is the sort who displays qualities you can't quite fathom. This is a similar situation to the small child presented with a musical box: he likes it, but can't see how it works, and likes it the more for that. In adult life, for an Aries, this occurs most often in meetings with Pisceans; the peculiar qualities of this liaison are explained more fully later, under Aries-Pisces relationships.

Arians don't need to marry for companionship; they are quite happy on their own. They don't need to marry for security or prestige; the former is an unknown concept to them anyway, and they generate their own prestige by achieving their own targets. Besides, prestige only exists in the eyes of others, and an Arian never thinks of the others, because he is self-centred, as we have noted before. Why, then, does an Arian marry at all?

An Arian's needs are all immediate; that is, he can see what he needs for now, but cannot see what he will need for the future. Besides, he is confident that he can meet the future when it comes. He may find that he needs a parent figure to give him a framework within which to operate, and to meet his daily needs. This person is likely to be his long-term partner. Once married he will put his energy into the family unit he has formed, and the whole group becomes driven by his force and energy. He devotes his time to making sure that his family is there at the top and in front, as well as himself. What the partner does best is direct the Arian's massive energy to the best use for the family, and comfort him when things go wrong. It only takes a little while for the Arian to recover his self-confidence, just as a child does, but during that time the Arian is convinced that nothing will ever go right again, because his powers have failed him; he doesn't know what else to try, and cannot take a view of things other than the immediate one. Consequently, the partner's job is one of comforter and supporter as well as being delighted by his energy and enthusiasm when all is well. The partner who combines all these qualities is rare, but that strange combination of co-adventurer, sparring partner, parent, and nurse is what any Arian looking for a marriage partner is trying to find.

Individual Compatibilities Sign by Sign

All relationships between the signs work in the ways described earlier in 'How Zodiacal Relationships Work' (page 35). In addition to that, descriptions of how an Arian attempts to form a relationship with someone from each of the twelve signs are given below. I have tried to show not what a Gemini, for example, is like, but what an Arian sees him as, and how he sees you. Each individual Gemini looks different, of course, but their motivation is the same, and these descriptions are meant to help you understand what you are trying to do with them, and how they are trying to handle you. As usual, the words he and his can be taken to mean she and her, since astrology makes no distinctions in sex here.

Aries-Aries
Like most of the relationships formed by two people of the same sign, this will tend to show the pair of you, not just how similar you are, but how much of yourself you don't like. Mars is the guiding principle here, of course, and it is not in his nature to give ground or assimilate another point of view.

An Arian has to push forwards the whole time, and the problem here is going to be making sure that the two of you are in fact pushing in the same direction; otherwise there will inevitably be stresses set up, and these will lead to friction and arguments. As long as the two of you are interested in the same things, there will be no problems. Progress will in fact be much more rapid than in other partnerships, because you have twice the motive power available, and because you will fuel each other's enthusiasm for as long as your interests stay together.

The weak point in all this is that neither of you is interested in the relationship as a thing in itself; doing something for the sake of the relationship alone, when it was of no interest or profit to you personally, is something that you never do, and of course, that applies to both of you.

Another problem area is that an Arian gets frustrated at lack of progress; he has no patience at all, and is particularly annoyed when this is due to someone doing just what he wanted to do, but doing it first. When someone thwarts him by being impatient, headstrong, imprudent, or just downright selfish, then that doubles his displeasure. As you can see, another Arian displaying 'me-first' behaviour to his face does nothing for an Arian's temper. Luckily, both of you will forget the incident and move on to something else in a very short time, so you may take comfort from the thought that disagreements between Arians are of short duration, with neither side holding grudges for long.

This double helping of Martian energy, with its tendency to extremes of enthusiasm and dislike, makes for a lively friendship which is likely to be punctuated by arguments at fairly frequent intervals. As a basis for a love affair, the same thing applies: the passions will be intense, and to some extent feed off each other to give an even greater intensity; quarrels will be violent, and quick to flare, but quick to cool again also. As time progresses with such a pairing, the intensity does not diminish, but the time scale extends somewhat; arguments take longer to arrive and to fade away, but the passion and intensity of both the arguments and the good times in between remains undiminished.

As a business partnership, Aries-Aries needs careful channelling; for best effect, indeed for any progress to be made at all, you must split the tasks between you, and each devote his full attention to his own tasks. Authority within your own appointed areas must be absolute, and on no account should you attempt to interfere in any way with your partner's side of things. If this partitioning is not adhered to, your energies will hinder and oppose each other sooner or later, and the resulting arguments are wasteful of time and energy for the business (which neither of you can actually see as an entity in itself, of course).

Aries-Taurus
On the face of it, this is probably the hardest of all the zodiacal

partnerships to make work well. The intensity and eagerness of the Arian is completely at odds with the more patient qualities of the Taurean.

Venus looks after Taurus, and that means that the underlying quality is one of stability and comfort; the Arian's Mars-given qualities, demanding new experiences and sometimes danger and hardship, have nothing in common with those of Venus. This seems hard enough, but the animosity is deeper still, and the reason has to do with the fact that the signs follow on from one another in the zodiacal sequence. Aries is always striving to make something for himself; he wants to be the one to discover, develop, and use something first, so that he can truly say that it is his very own thing, and that nobody else thought of it first. What does he do when this is achieved? He fears that he might be forced to settle down and look to his responsibilities, make sure his projects become mature and established, that sort of thing. Although this is the right way for things to develop, the Arian is afraid that in settling down he would become boring, and would never know the thrill of starting something new again. Taureans show this settled state in everything they do, and because it is the natural thing for an Aries to move forwards, being the next stage in the circle, so to speak, it becomes something to fear and dislike, since it involves giving up Arian-ness. The eternally forward-looking, childlike Aries doesn't like growing up any faster than he has to, and will avoid the whole process if he possibly can.

The same process applies to Taurus in reverse. It is part of a Taurean to value the ground he stands on; think of a bull in a field, and how he continually re-defines and guards his territory. Whatever a Taurean acquires he considers his own, and it is his duty to look after it. This means that a Taurean's 'territory' keeps getting bigger throughout his life, and he becomes less and less inclined to give any of it up. The idea of an Arian trampling all over it, changing it, trying to do something new and original with it, or worst of all, throwing it away to concentrate on something completely new that hasn't been tried before, horrifies him. The Taurean has already been through the energetic process of acquisition, and he much prefers the steady state of being in possession; because Arian energies are in the past to him, he finds them irritating and clichéd, which in turn enrages the Arian, to whom they are new and vivid, and who would like them appreciated as such.

If the friendship between these two is not very intellectual, then the relationship must eventually become a series of battles, where the Aries' temper and will to win causes the Taurean to dig his hooves in even deeper, refusing to move. Eventually the Taurean's anger, slow to build but unstoppable once it has got going, will explode, and the force of it will flatten even the Arian for a while. This sort of thing is dangerous for both of them. The Taurean's flat refusal to change in any way will frustrate the Arian even more, and the partnership is unlikely to develop.

With a little thought, however, a working agreement can be found, which will work well both in business and on a personal level. What needs to be achieved first, obviously, is an understanding of each other's needs. After that, things are best arranged so that the Arian does the active work and anything new and energetic, while the Taurean does the maintenance and the support duties for the team as a unit. In this way the Arian is spared the repetition and the inactive periods he so hates, and the Taurean has plenty to look after and consider his own.

The Arian must remember that the Taurean is possessive of him too, and will be extremely jealous if the Arian shows any interest in another partner; the Taurean must remember that Arians need to move around a bit to be at their best.

Aries-Gemini

Aries and Gemini were made for each other. The need for action in the one is matched by the need for novelty and stimulus in the other. As an Arian, you will find that the Gemini is much faster mentally than you are, and ready to move on to new challenges and new concepts almost as soon as you have arrived at them. You find all this stimulating, and relish being made to keep up, but you hope that it is all as honest as it seems to be, because you have a sneaking suspicion that the Gemini might be presenting things to you the wrong way round just for the fun of it, and you might not be quick enough to see through the deception. The trouble here is that Aries is a straightforward sort of sign, and lacks the subtlety of intellect required to play with words and ideas, to conjure fantasies from nowhere, and to make clever lies that live alongside the truth unable to be distinguished from it. Gemini, on the other hand, is almost pure intellect; everything is examined for its mental rather than physical qualities, and turned this way and that to see if it has anything interesting to offer when examined from a different point of view. Duplicity is easy for them; a Gemini is not fundamentally dishonest, but he loves arguments for their own sake, and he loves all forms of trickery.

You will not tire him out, nor he you; you have much greater physical capabilities than he does, and much more sheer strength, but his speed of reaction is phenomenal, and he uses himself much more sparingly. He does with reflexes what you do with muscle.

As a friendship, there is little to fault the pairing of these two signs; as a love match, things could turn out a little different. There is no lack of sexual compatibility; both of you enjoy any physical activity, and you will get extra pleasure from the laughter that the Gemini will bring to things. The trouble starts when the Arian falls in love; your simple and direct passion, when honestly and earnestly expressed, will amuse the Gemini, and he will turn his interest to something else. This isn't rejection; it's just that earnestness is a bit too serious for the Gemini mind, and the fun is taken out of anything for him when seriousness starts to creep in. Also, he needs variety; by the time you are getting serious about things, the relationship will have been going for some time, and he will be needing a change. If you can put up with his lightweight response and his refusal to be committed in any way, then things can continue almost indefinitely. He can provide you with a seemingly endless series of ideas and new projects, and you can explore them together. Just keep it light, and keep it moving.

In many ways, this one works best if kept at the level of two very close friends. You will never really understand or appreciate what goes on inside the Gemini's head, and how much he gets out of your adventures together; he will never believe what deep satisfaction you get out of using yourself physically, testing your own limits, doing something that nobody else has ever done, and experiencing it for yourself, first-hand. He would think such a notion absurdly over-dramatic and inflated, and prefers not to think of you, his best friend, in such terms. So you must stay side by side, moving in parallel, enjoying each other's company, and taking individual pleasures in different ways from the experiences you share. Kept like that, and kept light and active, the relationship is nearly perfect.

Aries-Cancer

This one seems the most unlikely partnership possible, but it can be surprisingly productive if approached in the right way, and the feature that surprises most of all is its *strength*.

Both of you have the Sun in cardinal signs; this means that you are both of the belief that if you don't do things for yourself, then they won't happen. This ability, and indeed need, to get things done for yourself is something you share, and you can recognize and respect it in each other.

You realize, both of you, that you are directing your energies in very different directions, but that these directions are not necessarily opposite. The Arian is keen to find things out for himself, by direct action; the Cancerian does not feel the need for this, but is very concerned that he is in control of all the things around him. Cancerians do not just put down roots, they actively dig foundations. They want to look after things, but that means looking after them their way, and making sure that the creative and directing energy to do that comes from them and them alone. It is this directing energy, and the belief that being in control of what you do is the only way to get it done the way you want it done, that the Arian can see and appreciate in the Cancerian, and it is the personal drive, energy and confidence in his abilities that appeal to the Cancerian when shown in the Arian.

This simple mutual appreciation of forcefulness is probably enough to turn an acquaintance into an affair; after all, the Arian can only show his admiration for the other's energies by physical demonstration, because he doesn't work any other way—and the Cancerian cannot but be flattered that someone as obviously sure and certain in his opinions as an Aries is directing his energies his way in recognition of similar qualities in himself.

The problem then becomes one of timing; Cancer has a much longer view than Aries, and is likely to be considering the affair as the preliminary groundwork for a much more lasting partnership. Marriage is always a possibility, if not a necessary condition, in a Cancerian relationship of any kind. There is always the element of protection and security built in to the notion of marriage, and a Cancer feels that this will help to fight any future events involving change and the unexpected, which would of course stop things being the way he wanted them. As an Aries, you feel that this over-reliance on security is a silly idea, and fail to give it the importance which it has in the eyes of your partner; you may also feel that marriage as a goal in a relationship is not quite what you go into these things for, and you would be right. That doesn't mean that it isn't what other people go into relationships for, though.

What you will realize, Aries, is that the Cancer will look after all those areas of your life that you know you should, but can't be bothered with. They will keep you on a firm footing, and that needn't necessarily mean tied down. They will look after your home and guard your interests in exactly the manner you would like to see someone doing—that is, with energy and confidence in their approach. In return, you can give them the appreciation they deserve, and be their public representative, using your personality and flair to do the jobs that their natural reserve prevents them from doing. You can be their public face, and they will be right behind you, making sure that everything is under control and has been looked after.

The nature of this relationship is that you fight for each other, on each other's behalf, and do the work for each other that you cannot do yourselves. There are bound to be arguments, since you both like doing things in your own way, but they will pass quickly. As a marriage, it will not be easy, but it will be strong, and it will be very productive.

Aries-Leo
The union of two signs of similar element, such as the two fire signs in this case, is usually taken to be a good thing. This is no exception, though there are one or two problems caused by our being *too* similar.

Both of you have a need to be number one. For you as an Arian, the emphasis is on doing things for yourself, and excelling at what you do; the Leo sees things a different way. For him, the emphasis is on being seen as leader, being recognized as the natural centre of things, to whom people turn for reassurance and warmth.

As you will realize, you are not likely to give a Leo the sort of respect he thinks he deserves if you think that you can do things any better, and this will undermine his position. If, on the other hand, you can't do things any better, and should therefore look to him for advice, you will see him as a rival and be forced to compete with him until you eventually surpass him; you see yourself as a natural leader, and you think your place is in front.

If you can realize that you are essentially similar in outlook, you can get along very well indeed. You are both active, in that you prefer to do things rather than be passive and wait for things to happen. You are both essentially outward-looking and optimistic, believing that things can, and probably will, improve. You have both got a lively sense of humour, with the Arian probably the sharper of the two, and you are both capable of giving out enough energy to inspire and help others who don't seem to be able to make it on their own.

Where you differ most is that the Arian needs to make his own territory, to go where others haven't been before and claim it for himself, whereas the Leo is much happier to find himself in an existing situation and put his energies into it from the inside. Eventually he becomes the central figure wherever he is, and becomes responsible for the general morale and social life of the group. It isn't important for the Leo to be seen doing the impossible or proving that he is the best; what is important is that he be recognized as such, and given the respect due to his position.

Provided that neither of you trespass on the other's territory, your bright and radiant personalities will attract each other without much effort from either party, and an affair could easily grow. This will be conducted with all the heat that Fire signs usually generate, and the warmth of the affection will be visible to outsiders, though it will not seem especially passionate to you, since you do everything with that sort of intensity. Emotions will be easily expressed, and in a simple manner, because both of you are surprisingly unsophisticated in your emotional requirements. You are both easily hurt, and will show that you are hurt—this is usually because you both want your own way at once, and one of you has been forced to take second place.

If you can learn to take second place once in a while, perhaps in turns, then a warm and lasting marriage is possible. You can be very good for each other, with the Aries learning the pleasure of giving to others, and the Leo learning that responding to challenges doesn't necessarily mean loss of prestige.

Aries-Virgo

In all relationships where the two Sun signs are five signs separated there is an element of adjustment to be found; that is, for the two people to work at all well together, they must be prepared to modify their usual point of view, for there is little, if any, common ground between them.

Aries is too forceful and immediate for Virgo; as an Arian, you will find that the Virgo's willingness, if not actual preference, to do the same things over and over again until familiarity is exceeded, drives you to distraction. It is enough for you to do something and get it right; it is often enough just to do it and get some sort of a successful outcome. Not so the Virgo; he likes to master the way of doing things as well as getting a result. Technique is important to him. Each time a Virgo does something it is not the same as before; he modifies his way of doing it, learns from it, understands more about the processes involved, and analyses all this in a way which is quite alien to the Arian way of thought.

If you have common interests, then you can approach them from your separate directions, and progress through each other's talents. You can be the driving force, and he can be the technique. You use his know-how and skill, but supply the enthusiasm and motivation yourself. Seen from the other point of view, the Virgo finds that he is saved from getting bogged down in small detail, and rescued from those times when he cannot provide the impetus to move forwards, by the Arian's eagerness to get things moving, and general vitality. There is always power and stamina on hand in the Aries character, and the Virgoan is grateful for it.

Because the Virgo is so careful, and needs time to analyse a new idea for a while before he commits himself to it, your way of throwing yourself into something because you feel good about it will meet with a less than equal response, and you must be ready for this if you find yourself emotionally involved with one. It's not that they don't respond, just that they need convincing that the affair is going to be the sort of thing that they'd like. They can take quite a bit of convincing at times, and are not to be won over by five minutes' impassioned protestation.

As business partners, they can be wonderful provided that both of you adapt your working style to take the other's strengths into account (the adjustment mentioned earlier). Virgoans can think of all the possibilities inherent in a business stratagem and use your energies to make them work; if you accuse him of being too picky, then you are throwing away his analytical talents, and exposing both of you to the sort of oversights that you yourself make through haste and over-eagerness. He must be prepared to make decisions in a once-and-for-all manner, and be prepared to take a few risks. If he doesn't, he loses all the advantages of your speed and talent for effective action. You must both be prepared to do things the other's way, and then things will go very well.

As marriage partners, Virgoans are very careful about the family's diet and general state of health, whereas you tend to eat anything you can find when you're hungry, because you need to provide fuel for all the energy you put out. There will be times when they seem to do things so very slowly, but you must just accept this, as they have to accept your rapid changes of mind and impassioned outbursts when things don't turn out just the way you want. To them, this looks like sheer carelessness and lack of planning, but they will forgive you.

Aries-Libra
This pairing is based on the attraction of opposites. In a nutshell, everything you do or feel is done in the opposite way by the Libran. That doesn't mean in terms of literally doing the opposite things, of course; but think of why you do something, the motivation behind it, and you will be able to observe the Libran doing things for the opposite reasons.

Librans are far less active than you are, and less decisive too. Where you want to do things for yourself, and rarely consider what anybody else might want to do, the Libran is always ready to listen to alternative points of view, and is quite likely to be swayed by any of them. He would much rather do something in company than on his own, which means that he is likely to find himself doing what his friends suggest, rather than be left out.

Your decisiveness will guide him easily; you decide what you want to do, and the Libran will agree. The benefit to you is that you have a companion, and the benefit to him is that somebody is taking the decisions for him, so that he doesn't have to think too hard. Librans can get very inactive and ineffective because they have an infinite capacity for putting things off until another time, and having an Arian partner will cure this. Of course, you have to be prepared to push them into action some of the time, and if you don't want any of that, then perhaps this relationship is not for you.

The problem in this particular coupling of zodiacal types is that you are both concerned with personal issues. If that sounds strange, think how much the Taurean is concerned with what he owns, or the Capricorn with his status—neither of them are bothered too much about themselves as *people*. You and the Libran are much more concerned with yourselves—you with being an individual, and the Libran with being a partner to somebody. Therefore the relationship between you has to be built on your personal relationship, and cannot rely on common interests such as your children, your careers, your shared possessions and activities, to succeed. You have to actually like each other. If the Libran feels that he isn't close enough to you, then he grows remote and dejected; if you feel that he is a weight round your neck, then you get angry and feel that you cannot be yourself on your own any more. As you can see, it is a tightrope existence, and you must both be very careful. All the 'opposite sign' relationships are like this, but yours is the only one which works at such a personal level.

In any relationship with a Libran, you are going to feel that their heart isn't in it; how else, you reason, could they account for being so slow to respond? You are seeing it from your own point of view, which is reasonable enough. The Libran wants to know how little things will be disrupted if he does something new; how much will things be the same as before? He is willing to give things a try, especially if you think it's a good idea, but he needs time to think about it, and will try to manage it so that there is very little disturbance of his usual routines. Once you realize that you are always going to be the one to make the moves, the one who wants things to happen at once, all will be well. Once the Libran realizes that being active isn't likely to throw him off balance, and that when he's finished being active he can sit down again in his favourite chair, things will be better yet.

Any long-term relationship between you, such as a marriage, or going into business together, is bound to be something of a see-saw arrangement, alternating between furious activity and periods of quiet. More than anything else, though, success in these long-term undertakings depends on your actually liking each other quite a lot.

Aries-Scorpio

This is the sort of relationship you always promised yourself—
somebody with the strength, drive, and pure sex-appeal to give
you a run for your money, test your strength and stamina, and
completely fulfil you.

The trouble is that it's not quite like that in real life. It can be,
but there is always more to it than that, and it's the 'more' part
that you're not too happy with. The plain truth is that a Scorpio
can give you more than you wanted.

You are both ruled by the planet Mars, and that's what
gives both of you the limitless reserves of energy you have. All
this energy needs physical expression at least, if not sexual
expression, and for the Arian it seems as though everyone else in
the Zodiac is a little dull and lifeless compared to the powerful
pulse of Mars he himself enjoys. Scorpio is the other, indeed the
only other, zodiacal sign with Mars as the driving force. The
difference between you is, quite simply, that while you are
motivated by being Mars, expressing it as a physical force, the
Scorpio is motivated by controlling Mars, using it as a powerful
tool.

The Scorpio has none of your instinctive belief that nothing
can go wrong because you will somehow be able to blaze your
way through your difficulties with a touch of luck and some
applied enthusiasm. For him nothing goes wrong because he
stays in control, and everything runs in the paths he thought it
would. The Martian energy is used to direct and control; he
needs to know how things work, what goes on in the background
while nobody else is looking, and how he can stay on top of it all
by pulling a few strings here and there. He is very emotional, and
his emotions run very deep; most of them are below the surface,
but he never stops thinking, and never stops feeling things
either, which most people forget. All the intensity of emotional
response which in you is on the surface, in him is there but
invisible. A chastening thought, isn't it?

Consequently, a love affair between you will be a very
powerful thing, stronger than you can imagine. You can only
imagine things on one level at a time, Aries; the Scorpio has no

limits. When a little trust has grown, you will be able to see some of his depths, but nothing like all of them. You will offer him your physical self, which is all you have to offer, and is the part which means most to you, and he will match your strength. If you are very strong, he may withdraw a little, because to lose to you would entail loss of control, which he cannot risk; there must always be a little bit left in reserve in a Scorpio—only you can play all out at once. He will control you, or try to, and he will be possessive, for to be otherwise would involve losing control; you may resent this, and fight him more fiercely than is good for either of you from time to time.

A Scorpio makes an admirable business partner, but you may not like the way he withholds information when it suits him, and how things seem to be going on over your head. An open sort of business relationship, one without secrets, is easier for you to grasp, and you feel happier there too, but you are unlikely to get one with a Scorpio. Still, they are very good indeed when it comes to making money grow.

Perhaps the passions and jealousies make this one a poor idea as a marriage partnership; it will certainly be up and down for most of the time. Best as an affair, I think.

Aries-Sagittarius

This is the last of the fire-to-fire groupings, and like the Leo partnership, you have a lot in common. This is the fire sign with the greatest mental capabilities; in fact, the greatest mental capabilities of all the twelve signs. Even brighter than the Gemini, and honest as well. The honesty of the Sagittarian, which shows itself to you, the Arian, as a bright kind of openness and optimism in speech, appeals to you. You cannot help but like a person who says what he thinks the moment he thinks it; he seems to have the same immediacy and delight in thought and speech as you have in action and movement, and he seems to get the same kind of pleasure from expressing it. All of this strikes you as very appealing, and you will be pleased to know that you are right to find it so. Sagittarians are very much a matter of 'What you see is what you get', and they are almost incapable of deception. So much so, in fact, that they are tactless in public, because they can't help telling it as they see it, and the honest truth spoken to someone's face often gives offence. Both you and the Sagittarian find this funny, and the two of you will be more convinced than ever that you are perfectly suited.

Basically, you find them inspirational. You will wish, when you have got to know them for a little while, that you could have just a little of their intellect, for which you would gladly trade some of your ease of movement and strength. This is because they dazzle you, to some extent, with their brilliant wit, their capacity for learning and remembering things, their fantastic imagination; they show you all this with such confidence and ease that you are over-impressed. Truth to tell, they show all these things to anybody, but it is the confidence and energy that appeals to you, because they seem to be speaking in your own language. They are: it is the language of the fire signs. Their tales sound terrifyingly risky to Cancerians, and woefully unplanned to Virgoans, but to you they sound like high adventure.

They find you wonderfully expressive of all their ideas. Sagittarians are changeable creatures, like their opposites, the Geminians; an idea only lasts as long as it takes for another one to replace it. Not so for you: once you have an idea, you make it work and make a success of it, and they find this very impressive. They appreciate your forcefulness, because they can never be anything for long; they love your self-assertive outlook, because it matches theirs, and they don't like dull company.

This changeable nature extends to their love affairs. It's not that they are purposefully cheating on you, but if somebody else seems attractive and available then their curiosity means that they have to give it a try. They will be genuinely apologetic afterwards, and would never willingly cause you any anguish, but they just can't resist the lure of something new, and they are going to do it next time, too, so be warned. You are likely to find this upsetting—not because you can't stand the competition, but because you can't stand the idea of being moved from the number one slot! They won't be able to see why you're so upset, which won't help at all. Whatever you do, though, don't demand loyalty: Sagittarians treat this as a serious attempt at curbing their freedom, and they will do anything to stay free. The more you insist, the more they will try to escape—and succeed, if the idea takes them.

As a long-term proposition, this partnership is very good indeed. A business venture between the pair of you will rise quickly, but you need to employ somebody else to look after the background work which neither of you enjoy, or you will have nothing beneath you, since you are both eager to be developing new areas of business without doing much to maintain the old ones. As a marriage, provided you recognize that your partner is going to need a bit of rope from time to time, and space to feel free in, you will have a friend for life who will be almost everything you ever wanted, and who will never fail to impress and amuse you.

Aries-Capricorn

The essential thing to remember about a Capricorn is that he is concerned first and foremost with what people think of him. If this doesn't meet with any understanding from you, then forget about any kind of relationship. Capricorns are devoted to getting on in life, so that they can be seen to be doing well. Status symbols were invented for, if not by, Capricorns. They all have high ambitions from an early age, and spend most of their lives working extremely hard so that these are achieved in one form or another. You can probably understand the idea of being number one; what you will have difficulty with is the desire to promote yourself at the expense of yourself. Think about that; a Capricorn doesn't mind hardship to himself as long as he gets what he wants, and he thinks that hard work is much too serious a thing to be enjoyed. The sheer pleasure of being you that runs through every vein of the Arian is not there in the Capricorn. This makes them, in your eyes, unimaginative, unfriendly, and dull.

If a Capricorn is interested in you, then you must ask yourself what he wants out of it, because his ambitions will still be in the forefront of his mind. He is likely to want your energy and ability to succeed first time; this last is something that he rarely accomplishes, because he just doesn't have the right way of attacking the problems, and he knows this. He recognizes your drive; it is similar to the drive of his own ambition, and he appreciates that. From your point of view, of course, you appreciate the things he has accomplished; you can admire a person who decides what he wants to do, and then goes out and does it. The pair of you, in fact, admire each other, but you can't understand why each of you does things in the manner you do. Most Aries-Capricorn relationships start off from mutual admiration.

You are likely to be the one who makes all the running in the relationship. If you are particularly wanting to find someone who cannot compete with your lively approach, then all is well, but most of you will find a Capricorn too careful, and emotionally reserved, which is not the way you work at all. In some cases, you may not be ambitious enough for them, especially if you are the sort of Arian who has a great time being himself, and doesn't really make any plans for the future. In this case the Capricorn will attempt to push you into doing things you don't much like, because if he doesn't he will feel that you are holding up his plans and not making best use of your energies for your joint future.

As a business partnership, it has much to recommend it, especially if you let the Capricorn do the organizing, and just address yourself to specific tasks one at a time. They will make sure you get the status you both deserve, and you will make sure he has the energy and drive he needs to bring his plans to fruition.

Aries-Aquarius

This is the sort of relationship that you like. It is similar in some ways to the Gemini link, in that the rapport is light and fast-moving, and your freedom to go your own way is not hindered in any way.

An Aquarian needs to form friendships; he feels that he works best in groups of people, and would much rather give his energies to the group than concentrate on his own ambitions. When you first meet an Aquarian, it is likely to be in a group, and in those surroundings they seem to be bright and attractive, somehow representing the best qualities of all the people present. That is exactly what they are doing, because they have put themselves into the group's identity, and taken that for their own character. On their own, Aquarians are shy and rather distant, and not particularly impressive. They need the warmth of friendship to make them work properly, and when that friend is someone as naturally fiery as you, their needs are met perfectly.

You need to have a friend who is there whenever you want them ,but is never going to close you in or attempt to tell you what to do. You also need a friend who is essentially kind and honest, because your own straightforward approach to life makes you easy meat for those whose outlook is less than scrupulous. As far as you are concerned, the Aquarian is just the job. They are by nature quite straight and fair in their dealings, and are unlikely to be trying to deceive you on purpose, though genuine misunderstandings can still occur, as in all relationships. Their relatively unemotional approach to life means that you are unlikely to meet strong opposition to your own ideas, and this means that you don't have to waste time and energy convincing your partner how right you are.

On the other hand, you may find that their lack of deeply felt passion about anything is a drawback. Perhaps you would like them to be a little more forceful. Try being boorish, unrefined, rude, or cruel and see where that gets you; an Aquarian cannot stand to see any of these qualities displayed, and will make quite sure that they are not displayed again, usually by getting other friends and associates to chastise you on their behalf. You won't see at first how the Aquarian works through people he knows, rather than directly; it never occurs to you that anybody could achieve anything in any other way than by themselves, but that's exactly how the Aquarian does things. They will change your tastes, too, moderating your excesses and turning your physical grace into social grace, your childishness into charm, and your will to win into inspired leadership.

What they get out of it is your warmth; the never-failing

enthusiasm and passion for things that take your fancy captivates them, and if they are the thing that you fancy, then they feel warmed, loved, and rewarded. An Aquarian cannot love himself, not deep down; he needs others to love him before he feels content.

As a partnership for business, it has everything to recommend it; they will be full of new schemes, and different ones, too, for they have a talent for the unusual which will surprise you. Their capacity for making contacts 'in the trade' is unparalleled. Make sure that you don't rush in and destroy the delicate networks of communication and cooperation that they set up just because you want something done immediately, and have become impatient.

Marriage could be a rarer event than you might imagine. Arians like to go their own way, and an Aquarian isn't going to try to tie you down. Aquarians are also solitary creatures from time to time, and there are times when they like their own company best, because constant emotional interchange is tiring for them. Marriage seems too restricting for the pure Arian, and too tiring for the pure Aquarian; other factors will have to make you tie the knot. Once married, though, you can be sure of a light and bright partnership, full of affection, if not very passionate; there will be plenty of variety, and challenges will be taken up and met rather than avoided. You could do worse.

Aries-Pisces

This is an odd partnership; like the Aries-Taurus one, it brings two adjacent signs in the zodiac into confrontation, and each of them then sees what he is, what he could be, and what he fears.

This time the other sign, Pisces, is behind you in the zodiacal circle, and thus represents all the things you secretly fear. Do you want to have a relationship with somebody whose motivation is to exhibit and promote those qualities which worry you?

I know you are thinking that there is nothing which really worries you, but there is. You are quite sure that in a definite situation you can apply your directness of mind and physical approach to get things going the way you want, but what if the situation were indefinite? What if it had nothing that was certain, nothing you could be sure of, nothing static or dependable? Now you begin to see what I mean. You represent a focus of energy, a point where things happen and take form. Pisces represents defocusing, a nowhere-in-particular that is everywhere at once, where everything is possible, but nothing is definite.

Pisceans are, therefore, people of infinite flexibility, who can take up any cause or put on any appearance they wish, according to the circumstances they find themselves in. If you are playing strong and sexy, they will too. If you are playing active and sporty, they will change to suit. They will reflect and complement you, and you will find that attractive.

Pisceans long for a definite thing to be; they wish that they could be as firm and effective as you are—for a while. Consequently they see in you a desirable state, and make themselves like that to amuse themselves and to please you. You will notice the differences, though; the Piscean will never learn to concentrate on the moment, his whole being given to the immediate present; instead, he exists in a sort of no-time, where everything is immediate, but the future has the same immediacy as the past. You, of course, don't have much of a sense of future time at all. More than that, you will notice how the Piscean reacts to obstacles. Challenges are something to meet as far as you're concerned, but to him they are to be avoided. Whenever difficulties arise, the Piscean melts away, makes himself scarce, flows round them; he reappears when the problem has been removed.

As business partners, it is very difficult to make this one work, unless you are in something connected with the media or the arts, where you make the impact and the Piscean supplies the sensitivity and imagination. As a marriage, then the understanding and tolerance that comes with time is the only answer, because you are very unlike. You might learn to enjoy uncertainty of mind, and your partner might learn to appreciate the practical advantages of decisive action. As lovers, it is an interesting experience for both of you, but possibly no more than that; you will be taken on flights of fantasy where nothing seems real (and you must remember that none of it is), and they will be invited to play games where strength and passion are the preferred currency. Dungeons and Dragons, perhaps?

Part 3
Your Life

5. The Year within Each Day

You have probably wondered, in odd moments, why there are more than twelve varieties of people. You know more than twelve people who look completely different. You also know more than one person with the same Sun sign as yourself who doesn't look anything like you. You also know two people who look quite like each other, but who are not related, and do not have birthdays near each other, so can't be of the same Sun sign. You will have come to the conclusion that Sun signs and astrology don't work too well, because anyone can see that there are more than twelve sorts of people.

You will also have wondered, as you finished reading a newspaper or magazine horoscope, how those few sentences manage to apply to a twelfth of the nation, and why it is that they are sometimes very close to your true circumstances, and yet at other times miles off. You will have come to the conclusion that astrology isn't all that it might be, but some of it is, and that you like it enough to buy magazines for the horoscopes, and little books like this one.

It might be that there is some other astrological factor, or factors, which account for all the different faces that people have, the similarities between people of different Sun signs, and the apparent inconsistencies in magazine horoscopes. There are, indeed, lots of other astrological factors we could consider, but one in particular will answer most of the inconsistencies we have noticed so far.

It is the Ascendant, or rising sign. Once you know your Ascendant, you will see how you get your appearance, your way of working, your tastes, your preferences and dislikes, and your state of health (or not, as the case may be). It is perhaps of more use to you to consider yourself as belonging to your Ascendant sign, than your Sun sign. You have been reading the wrong newspaper horoscopes for years; you are not who you thought you were!

You are about to protest that you know when your birthday is. I'm sure you do. This system is not primarily linked to your birthday, though. It is a smaller cogwheel in the clockwork of the heavens, and we must come down one level from where we have been standing to see its movements. Since astrology is basically the large patterns of the sky made small in an individual, there are a number of 'step-down' processes where the celestial machinery adjusts itself to the smaller scale of mankind; this is one of them.

Here's the theory:

Your birthday pinpoints a particular time during the year. The Sun appears to move round the strip of sky known as the zodiac during the course of the year. In reality, of course, our planet, Earth, moves round the Sun once a year, but the great friendly feature of astrology is that it always looks at things from our point of view; so, we think we stand still, and the Sun appears to move through the zodiac. On a particular day of importance, such as your birthday, you can see which of the zodiac signs the Sun is in, pinpoint how far it has gone in its annual trip round the sky, and then say 'This day is important to me, because it is my birthday; therefore this part of the sky is important to me because the Sun is there on my special day. What are the qualities of that part of the Sun's journey through the zodiac, and what are they when related to me?' The answer is what you usually get in a horoscope book describing your Sun sign.

Fine. Now let's go down one level, and get some more detail. The Earth rotates on its own axis every day. This means that, from our point of view, we stand still and the sky goes round us once a day. Perhaps you hadn't thought of it before, but that's how the Sun appears to move up and across the sky from sunrise to sunset. It's actually us who are moving, but we see it the other way round. During any day, then, your birthday included, the whole of the sky goes past you at some time or another; but at a particular moment of importance, such as the time that you were born, you can see where the Sun is, see which way up the sky is, and say, 'This moment is important to me, because I was born at this time; therefore the layout of the sky has the same qualities as I do. What are the qualities of the sky at this time of day, and what are they when related to me?'

You can see how you are asking the same questions one level lower down. The problem is that you don't know which bit of the sky is significant. Which bit do you look at? All you can see? All that you can't (it's spherical from your point of view, and has no joins; half of it is below the horizon, remember)?

How about directly overhead? A very good try; the point in the zodiac you would arrive at is indeed significant, and is used a lot by astrologers, but there is another one which is more useful still. The eastern horizon is the point used most. Why? Because it fulfils more functions than any other point. It gives a starting point which is easily measurable, and is even visible (remember, all astrology started from observations made before mathematics or telescopes). It is also the contact point between the sky and the earth, from our point of view, and thus symbolizes the relationship between the sky and mankind on the earth. Finally, it links the smaller cycle of the day to the larger one of the year, because the Sun starts its journey on the eastern horizon each day as it rises; and, if we are concerned with a special moment, such as the time of your birth, then the start of the day, or the place that it started, at any rate, is analogous to the start of your life. Remember that you live the qualities of the moment you were born for all of your life; you are that moment made animate.

The point in the zodiac, then, which was crossing the eastern horizon at the time you were born, is called the Ascendant. If this happened to be somewhere in the middle of Gemini, then you have a Gemini Ascendant, or Gemini rising, whichever phrase you prefer. You will see that this has nothing to do with the time

Different signs are on the horizon at different times according to where you live, as you can see. This is because of the difference in latitude. If you live in between the places given, you can make a guess from the values here. To compensate for longitude, subtract twelve minutes from your birthtime if you live in Glasgow, Liverpool or Cardiff; ten minutes for Edinburgh or Manchester; and six minutes for Leeds, Tyneside, or the West Midlands. *Add* four minutes for Norwich.

of year that you were born, only with the time of day.

Have a look at the diagrams on page 68, which should help explain things. If two people are born on the same day, but at different times, then the Ascendant will be different, and the Sun and all the other planets will be occupying different parts of the sky. It makes sense to assume, then, that they will be different in a number of ways. Their lives will be different, and they will look different. What they will have in common is the force of the Sun in the same sign, but it will show itself in different ways because of the difference in time and position in the sky.

How do you know which sign was rising over the eastern horizon when you were born? You will have to work it out. In the past, the calculation of the Ascendant has been the subject of much fuss and secrecy, which astrologers exploit to the full, claiming that only they can calculate such things. It does take some doing, it is true, but with a few short cuts and a calculator it need only take five minutes.

Here is the simplest routine ever devised for you to calculate your own Ascendant, provided that you know your time of birth. Pencil your answers alongside the stages as you go, so you know where you are.

1. Count forwards from 21 March to your birthday: 21 March is 1, 22 March is 2, and so on.
2. Add 182 to this. New total is: .184...........................
3. Divide by 365, and then
4. Multiply by 24. Answer is now: ..12.09...........................
    (Your answer by now is between 0 and 24. If it isn't, you have made a mistake somewhere. Go back and try again).
5. Add your time of birth, in 24-hour clock time. If you were born at 3 p.m., that means 15. If you were born in Summer Time, take one hour off. If there are some spare minutes, your calculator would probably like them in decimals, so it's 0.1 of an hour for each six minutes. 5.36 p.m. is 17.6, for example. Try to be as close as you can. New total is: .20 : 0.1.....

6. If your total exceeds 24, subtract 24. Your answer must now be between 0 and 24. Answer is: . . . .

7. You have now got the time of your birth not in clock time, but in sidereal, or star, time, which is what astrologers work in. Page 68 has a strip diagram with the signs of the zodiac arranged against a strip with the values 0 to 24, which are hours in star time. Look against the time you have just calculated, and you will see which sign was rising at the time you were born. For example, if your calculated answer is 10.456, then your Ascendant is about the 16th degree of Scorpio.

What Does the Ascendant Do?

Broadly speaking, the Ascendant does two things. Firstly, it gives you a handle on the sky, so that you know which way up it was at the time you entered the game, so to speak; this has great significance later on in the book, when we look at the way you handle large areas of activity in your life such as your career, finances, and ambitions. Secondly, it describes your body. If you see your Sun sign as your mentality and way of thinking, then your Ascendant sign is your body and your way of doing things. Think of your Sun sign as the true you, but the Ascendant as the vehicle you have to drive through life. It is the only one you have, so you can only do with it the things of which it is capable, and there may be times when you would like to do things in a different way, but it 'just isn't you'. What happens over your life is that your Sun sign energies become specifically adapted to express themselves to their best via your Ascendant sign, and you become an amalgam of the two. If you didn't, you would soon become very ill. As an Arian with, say, a Gemini Ascendant, you do things from an Arian motivation, but in a Gemini way, using a Gemini set of talents and abilities, and a Gemini body. The next few sections of the book explain what this means for each of the Sun/Ascendant combinations.

Some note ought to be made of the correspondence between the Ascendant and the actual condition of the body. Since the

Ascendant sign represents your physical frame rather than the personality inside it, then the appearance and well-being of that frame is also determined by the Ascendant sign. In other words, if you have a Libra Ascendant, then you should look like a Libran, and you should be subject to illnesses in the parts of the body with a special affinity to that sign.

The Astrology of Illness

This is worth a book in itself, but it is quite important to say that the astrological view of illness is that the correlation between the individual and the larger universe is maintained. In other words, if you continue over a long period of time with a way of behaviour that denies the proper and necessary expression of your planetary energies, then the organ of your body which normally handles that kind of activity for your body systems will start to show the stresses to you. A simple example: Gemini looks after the lungs, which circulate air, and from which oxygen is taken all over the body. Gemini people need to circulate among a lot of people, talking and exchanging information. They act as the lungs of society, taking news and information everywhere. They need to do this to express their planetary energies, and society needs them to do this or it is not refreshed, and does not communicate. You need your lungs to do this, too. Lungs within people, Geminis within society: same job, different levels. If you keep a Gemini, or he keeps himself, through circumstance or ignorance, in a situation where he cannot talk or circulate, or where he feels that his normal status is denied, then he is likely to develop lung trouble. This need not be anything to do with a dusty atmosphere, or whether he smokes, although obviously neither of those will help; they are external irritants, and this is an internal problem caused by imbalance in the expression of the energies built into him since birth. In the sections which follow, all the observations on health are to do with how the body shows you that certain behaviour is unbalancing you and causing unnecessary stress; problems from these causes are alleviated by listening to yourself and changing your behaviour.

Your Ascendant

Aries Ascendant

If you have Aries rising as well as the Sun in Aries, you are an uncommon individual, because Aries only rises for about fifty minutes out of the twenty-four hour day. You must have been born at about sunrise, or else you have got your sums wrong somewhere.

What you are trying to do with yourself is project an Arian personality through an Arian vehicle. You therefore end up with a much more intense display of Arian characteristics than other Arians, because you don't have to modify those inner energies in any way before the Ascendant can mobilize them. You will always be trying to do things faster than anybody else, and this can lead to hastiness and a certain degree of accident-proneness. What you see as the correct way to do things involves immediate action by the most direct method, to secure instant, and measurable, results. You feel that unless you are directly and personally responsible for doing things, then they cannot be done, not only because you believe that only you can do them properly, but because you get no satisfaction from letting anybody else do anything. Personal experience of everything is the only way you learn; reading about it, or watching it, does nothing for you.

You are likely to have headaches as a recurring problem if you push yourself too hard, and you should watch your blood pressure too. Mars, ruling Aries, is a strong and forceful planet, and it is bound to get you a little over-stressed at times. You are also likely to have problems digesting things properly. Astrologically, all illnesses apply to your external condition as well as your internal condition, so think carefully; when your head aches you are banging it too hard against a problem which cannot be overcome that way, and when you are not digesting properly, you have not understood the implications of what you have taken on. In both cases, allow time to think and consider.

Taurus Ascendant

You were born at about breakfast time if you have Taurus rising, and that fits quite well with the Taurean's well known liking for food. You are still Arian, of course, but you do things in a Taurean way, and with a Taurean body as your vehicle. You should look Taurean: quite thick-set, big around the neck and shoulders sometimes, and with large hands. You should have a broad mouth, and large eyes, which are very attractive. You should also have a good voice—not only as a singing voice, but one which is pleasant to listen to in conversation too.

The Taurean method for getting things done is to look forward to, and then enjoy, the material reward for one's efforts. It is part of Taurean thinking that if you can't touch it, buy it, own it or eat it, it isn't real and it isn't worth much. You will also be concerned to keep what is yours, not to waste your energies on what won't gain you anything or increase your possessions, and not to attempt anything which you don't think you have more than a chance of achieving.

Taureans do have taste; not only taste for food, which they love, but artistic taste, which they develop as a means of distinguishing things of value which they would then like to acquire and gain pleasure from owning. Unlike the Capricorn way of doing things, which values quality because it is valued by others, Taureans enjoy their possessions for themselves. The drawback to the Taurean approach is the lack of enterprise, and the unwillingness to try things just for the fun of it.

Taurean Ascendant people have throat and glandular problems, and all problems associated with being overweight. They can also have back and kidney problems caused as a result of an unwillingness to let things go in their external life. A lighter touch is needed in the approach to problems of possession; shedding unwanted or outworn things in a desirable process.

Gemini Ascendant

If you have a Gemini Ascendant you were born mid-morning. You should have expressive hands and a wide range of gestures which you use as you speak (ask your friends!) and you are perhaps a little taller than average, or than other members of your family. Gemini Ascendant people also have dark hair, if there is any possibility of it in their parents' colouring, and quick, penetrating eyes which flash with amusement and mischief; Gemini Ascendant women have very fine eyes indeed.

The Gemini approach to things, which you find yourself using, is one in which the idea of a thing is seen as being the most useful, and in which no time must be lost in telling it to other people so that they can contribute their own ideas and responses to the discussion. The performance of the deed is of no real importance in the Gemini view; somebody else can do that. Ideas and their development are what you like to spend time on, and finding more people to talk to, whose ideas can be matched to your own, seems to you to offer the most satisfaction.

There are two snags to the Gemini approach. The first is that there is a surface quality to it all, in which the rough outline suffices, but no time is spent in development or long-term experience. It may seem insignificant, but there is some value in seeing a project through to the end. The second snag is similar, but is concerned with time. The Gemini approach is immediate, in that it is concerned with the present or the near future. It is difficult for a Gemini Ascendant person to see farther than a few months into the future, if that; it is even more difficult for him to extend his view sideways in time to see the impact of his actions on a wider scene. Both of these things he will dismiss as unimportant.

Gemini Ascendant people suffer from chest and lung maladies, especially when they cannot communicate what they want to or need to, or when they cannot circulate socially in the way that they would like. They also have problems eliminating wastes from their bodies, through not realizing the importance of ending things as well as beginning them. In both cases, thinking and planning on a broader scale than usual, and examination of the past to help make better use of the future, is beneficial.

Cancer Ascendant
You were born around noon if you have a Cancer Ascendant and

an Aries Sun and this will make for great success in your chosen career, whatever it is. Whatever the job title is, Arians actually do what they want and please themselves anyway, so being born around the middle of the day simply guarantees public prominence and makes it that much swifter to arrive.

The Cancerian frame, through which you project your Arian energies, may mean that you appear a little round and not so muscular as other Arians. Your energies are in no way diminished; in fact, you are likely to be even more determined, and be described in newspaper clichés like 'small and soft to look at, but with a will of steel'. Your face could be almost cherubic and you could have small features in a pale complexion with grey eyes and brown hair. The key to the Cancer frame is that it is paler than usual, less well defined, and has no strong colouring. Strong noses and red hair do not come from a Cancerian Ascendant.

The Cancerian approach to things is highly personal. All general criticisms are taken personally, and all problems in any procedure for which they have responsibility are seen as a personal failing. As an Arian with a Cancerian way of working, you will be concerned to use your energies for the safe and secure establishment of things from the foundations up, so that you know that whatever you have been involved in has been done properly, and is unlikely to let you down in any way; you are concerned for your own safety and reputation. The other side of this approach is that you can be a little too concerned to make sure everything is done personally, and be unwilling to entrust things to other people. Not only does this overwork you, it seems obsessive and uncooperative to others.

The Cancer Ascendant person has health problems with the maintenance of the flow of fluids in his body, and a tendency to stomach ulcers caused by worry. Cancer Ascendant women should pay special attention to their breasts, since the affinity between the sign, the Moon as ruler of all things feminine, and that particular body system means that major imbalances in the life are likely to show there first. There could also be some problems with the liver and the circulation of the legs; the answer is to think that, metaphorically, you do not have to support everybody you know: they can use their own legs to stand on, and you do not have to feed them either.

Leo Ascendant

Early afternoon saw your arrival in the world if you have Leo as an Ascendant sign. Leo, as the determinant of the physical character-istics, makes itself known by the lion of the sign—you can always spot the deep chest, proud and slightly pompous way of walking, and, more often than not, the hair arranged in some sort of a mane, either full or taken back off the face, and golden if possible. Leo Ascendant people have strong voices and a definite presence to them. Aries Sun and Leo Ascendant will bring to the fore any hereditary tendency to golden or red colouring, so a flushed complexion, or coppery hair, or even freckles, may be in evidence.

The Leonine way of doing things is to put yourself in the centre and work from the centre outwards, making sure that everybody knows where the commands are coming from. It is quite a tiring way of working; you need to put a lot of energy into it, because you are acting as the driving force for everybody else. Preferred situations for this technique are those where you already know, more or less, what's going to happen; this way you are unlikely to be thrown off balance by unexpected develop-ments. The grand gesture belongs to the Leo method; it works best if all processes are converted into theatrical scenes, with roles acted rather than lived. Over-reaction, over-dramatization, and over-indulgence are common, but the approach is in essence kind-hearted and well-meant. Children enjoy being with Leo Ascendant people, and they enjoy having children around them. The flaws in the approach are only that little gets done in difficult circumstances where applause and appreciation are scarce commodities, and that little is attempted that is really new and innovatory.

The health problems of the Leo Ascendant person come from the heart, and also from the joints, which suffer from mobility problems. These both come from a lifetime of being at the centre of things and working for everybody's good, and from being too stiff and unwilling to try any change in position. The remedy, of course, is to be more flexible, and to allow your friends to repay the favours they owe you.

Virgo Ascendant

A mid-afternoon birth puts Virgo on the Ascendant. Physically, this should make you slim and rather long, especially in the body; even if you have broad shoulders you will still have a long waist. There is a neatness to the features, but nothing notable; hair is brown, but again nothing notable. The nose and chin are often well-defined, and the forehead is often both tall and broad; the voice can be a little shrill and lacks penetration.

The Virgoan Ascendant person does not have an approach to life; he has a *system*. He analyses everything and pays a lot of attention to the way in which he works. It is important to the person with Virgo rising not only to be effective, but to be efficient; you can always interest them in a new or better technique. They watch themselves work, as if from a distance, all the while wondering if they can do it better. They never mind repetition; in fact they quite enjoy it, because as they get more proficient they feel better about things. An Arian with a Virgo Ascendant will want to know how anything and everything works; you will not be able to take anything for granted, and will have to devote all your attention to things until you have mastered their intricacies for yourself. There is a willingness to help others, to be of service through being able to offer a superior technique, inherent in the Virgo way of doing things, which prevents Virgo rising people from being seen as cold and unfriendly. They appreciate their help being appreciated. The problems in the Virgo attitude are a tendency to go into things in more detail than is necessary, and to be too much concerned with the 'proper' way to do things.

People with a Virgo Ascendant are susceptible to intestinal problems and circulatory problems, and may be prone to poor sight. All of these are ways in which the body registers the stresses of being too concerned with digesting the minutiae of things which are meant to be passed through anyway, and by not getting enough social contact. The remedy is to lift your head from your workbench sometimes, admit that the act is sometimes more important than the manner of its performance, and not to take things too seriously.

Libra Ascendant

You were born towards sunset if you have Libra rising; it will soften the impact of your Arianism on others. You should be tallish, and graceful, as all Libra Ascendant people tend to be, and have a clear complexion, and often blue eyes, set in an oval face with finely-formed features.

The Libra Ascendant person has to go through life at a fairly relaxed pace. The sign that controls his body won't let him feel rushed or anxious; if that sort of thing looks likely, then he will slow down a little until the panic's over. There is a need to see yourself reflected in the eyes of others, and so you will form a large circle of friends. You define your own opinion of yourself through their responses to you, rather than being sure what you want, and not caring what they think. Aries Sun, Libra Ascendant is going to make you eager to impress so that you can see the impact of your own energies on others. The more impressed they are, the better you'll feel. You will need to feel that they find you indispensable, although it is far more likely that they will find you irrepressible instead, and sometimes irritating.

The drawback to the Libran approach is that unless you have approval from others, you are unlikely to do anything on your own initiative, or at least you find it hard to decide on a course of action. You always want to do things in the way which will cause the least bother to anyone, and to produce an acceptable overall result; sometimes this isn't definite enough, and you need to know what you do want as well as what you don't.

The Libran Ascendant makes the body susceptible to all ailments of the kidneys and of the skin; there may also be trouble in the feet. The kidney ailments are from trying to take all the problems out of life as you go along. Sometimes it's better to attack a few of the obstacles and knock them flat in pure rage.

Scorpio Ascendant

You were probably born just after sunset if you have Scorpio for your Ascendant sign. It should give you a dark and powerful look, with a solid build, though not necessarily over-muscled, Scorpio Ascendant people tend to have a very penetrating and level way of looking at others, which is often disconcerting. Any possible darkness in the colouring is usually displayed, with dark complexions and dark hair, often thick and curly, never fine.

The Scorpio Ascendant person usually does things in a controlled manner. He is not given to explosive releases of energy unless they are absolutely necessary; even then, not often. He knows, or feels (a better word, since the Scorpionic mind makes decisions as a result of knowledge gained by feeling rather than thinking), that he has plenty of energy to spare, but uses it in small and effective doses, each one suited to the requirements of the task at hand. It does not seem useful to him to put in more effort than is strictly necessary for any one activity; that extra energy could be used somewhere else. The idea that overdoing things for their own sake is sometimes fun because of the sheer exhilaration of the release of energy does not strike a responsive chord in the Scorpio body, nor even much understanding. There is, however, understanding and perception of a situation which exists at more than one level. If anything is complicated, involving many activities and many people, with much interaction and many side issues which must be considered, then the Scorpio Ascendant person sees it all and understands all of it, in its minutest detail. They feel, and understand, the responses from all of their surroundings at once, but do not necessarily feel involved with them unless they choose to make a move. When they do move, they will have the intention of transforming things, making them different to conform to their ideas of how things need to be arranged.

Scorpio Ascendant people are unable simply to possess and look after anything; they must change it and direct it their way, and this can be a disadvantage.

Scorpio illnesses are usually to do with the genital and

excretory systems; problems here relate to a lifestyle in which things are thrown away when used, or sometimes rejected when there is still use in them. It may be that there is too much stress on being the founder of the new, and on organizing others; this will bring head pains, and illnesses of that order. The solution is to take on the existing situation as it is, and look after it without changing any of it.

Sagittarius Ascendant
It must have been well into the evening when you were born for you to have a Sagittarius Ascendant. If you have, you should be taller than average, with a sort of sporty, leggy look to you; you should have a long face with pronounced temples (you may be balding there if you are male), a well-coloured complexion, clear eyes, and brown hair. A Grecian nose is sometimes a feature of this physique.

The Sagittarian Ascendant gives a way of working that is based on mobility and change. This particular frame can't keep still and is much more comfortable walking than standing, more comfortable lounging or leaning than sitting formally. You tend to be in a bit of a hurry; travelling takes up a lot of your time, because you enjoy it so. It is probably true to say that you enjoy the process of driving more than whatever it is that you have to do when you get there. You probably think a lot of your car, and you are likely to have one which is more than just a machine for transport—you see it as an extension, a representation even, of yourself. People will notice how outgoing and friendly you seem to be, but they will need to know you for some time before they realize that you enjoy meeting people more than almost anything else, and you dislike being with the same companions all the time. There is a constant restlessness in you; you will feel that being static is somehow unnatural, and it worries you. You are an optimist, but can also be an opportunist, in that you see no reason to stay doing one thing for a moment longer than it interests you. The inability to stay and develop a situation or give long-term commitment to anything is the biggest failing of this sign's influence.

A person with Sagittarius rising can expect to have problems with his hips and thighs, and possibly in his arterial system; this is to do with trying to leap too far at once, in all senses. You may also have liver and digestive problems, again caused by haste on a long-term scale. The remedy is to shorten your horizons and concentrate on things nearer home.

Capricorn Ascendant
It would have been around midnight when you were born for you to have a Capricorn Ascendant. This sign often gives a small frame, quite compact and built to last a long time, the sort that doesn't need a lot of feeding and isn't big enough or heavy enough to break when it falls over. The face can be narrow and the features small; often the mouth points downwards at the corners, and this doesn't change even when the person smiles or laughs.

The Capricorn sees life as an ordered, dutiful struggle. There is a great deal of emphasis placed on projecting and maintaining appearances, both in the professional and the personal life; the idea of 'good reputation' is one which everybody with Capricorn rising, whatever their sun sign, recognizes at once. There is a sense of duty and commitment which the Sagittarian Ascendant simply cannot understand; here the feeling is that there are things which need doing, so you just have to set to and get them done. Capricorn Ascendant people see far forwards in time, anticipating their responsibilities for years to come, even if their Sun sign does not normally function this way; in such cases they apply themselves to one problem at a time, but can envisage a succession of such problems, one after another, going on for years.

The disadvantages of this outlook are to do with its static nature. There is often a sense of caution that borders on the paranoid, and while this is often well disguised in affluent middle-class middle age, it seems a little odd in the young. This tends to make for a critical assessment of all aspects of a new venture before embarking on it, and as a result a lot of the original impetus is lost. This makes the result less than was originally hoped in many cases, and so a cycle of disappointment and unadventurousness sets in, which is difficult to break. The Capricorn Ascendant person is often humourless, and can seem determined to remain so.

These people have trouble in their joints, and break bones from time to time, entirely as a result of being inflexible. On a small scale this can be from landing badly in an accident because the Capricorn Ascendant keeps up appearances to the very end, refusing to believe that an accident could be happening to him: on a large scale, a refusal to move with the times can lead to the collapse of an outmoded set of values when they are swept away by progress, and this breaking up of an old structure can also cripple. They can get lung troubles, too, as a result of not taking enough fresh air, or fresh ideas. The best treatment is to look after their families rather than their reputation, and to think about the difference between stability and stagnation.

Aquarius Ascendant

Having an Aquarius Ascendant means that you were born in the early hours of the morning. This will make you chattier than you would otherwise have been, with a strong interest in verbal communication. There is a certain clarity, not to say transparency, about the Aquarian physique. It is usually tall, fair, and well shaped, almost never small or dark. There is nothing about the face which is particularly distinctive; no noticeable colouring, shape of nose, brows, or any other feature. It is an average sort of face, cleanly formed and clear.

The person with an Aquarian Ascendant wants to be independent. Not violently so, not the sort of independence that fights its way out of wherever it feels it's been put, just different from everybody else. Aquarius gives your body the ability to do things in ways perhaps not done before; you can discover new techniques and practices for yourself, and don't need to stay in the ways you were taught. There is a willingness to branch out, to try new things; not a Scorpionic wish to make things happen the way you want, but an amused curiosity which would just like to see if things are any better done a different way. There is no need for you to convince the world that your way is best: it only needs to suit you.

Of course, an Aquarian needs to measure his difference against others, and therefore you feel better when you have a few friends around you to bounce ideas off, as well as showing them how you're doing things in a slightly different way. You function best in groups, and feel physically at ease when you're not the only person in the room. You are not necessarily the leader of the group; just a group member. Group leaders put their energy into the group, and you draw strength and support from it, so you are unlikely to be the leader, though paradoxically all groups work better for having you in them.

A handicap arising from an Aquarian Ascendant is that you are unlikely to really feel passionately involved with anything, and this may mean that unless you have support from your friends and colleagues you will be unable to muster the determination necessary to overcome really sizeable obstacles in your chosen career.

You are likely to suffer from diseases of the circulation and in your lower legs and ankles; these may reflect a life where too much time is spent trying to be independent, and not enough support is sought from others. You may also get stomach disorders and colds because you are not generating enough heat: get more involved in things and angrier about them!

Pisces Ascendant

You were born an hour or so before sunrise if you have Pisces rising. Like Aries rising, Pisces is only possible as an Ascendant for about fifty minutes, so there aren't many of you around. Pisces Ascendant people are on the small side, with a tendency to be a bit pale and fleshy. They are not very well coordinated and so walk rather clumsily, despite the fact that their feet are often large. They have large, expressive, but rather sleepy-looking eyes.

As an Aries with Pisces rising, you will be very concerned to put yourself first. Although energetic, as those of your Sun sign normally are, the energy is not directed outwards for its own sake, as is usually the case, but in a strong reaction to reassert yourself in the face of whatever you experience. You will be very sensitive to all sorts of stimuli, and will react to them in an immediate way, since they will all strike you as equally important. This will give the appearance, from the outside at least, of either a touchy hostility, or an inability to concentrate on any one thing. You will prefer to be in an environment which offers variety, because the changing circumstance it offers will enable you to express your energies in many different ways according to how the mood takes you. Predictable surroundings will cause you to retire into your own imagination for amusement.

The major problem with a Pisces Ascendant is the inability to be active rather than reactive; to you there are too many possibilities for a single one to be decided upon. True, with an Aries Sun this tendency is lessened and once you have decided to act you will at least be effective in your action, but you will still be reacting to outside influences rather than generating your own movements from within yourself.

A Piscean Ascendant gives problems with the feet and the lymphatic system; this has connections with the way you move in response to external pressures, and how you deal with things which invade your system from outside. You may also suffer from faint-heartedness—literally as well as metaphorically. The remedy is to be more definite and less influenced by opinions other than your own.

6. Three Crosses: Areas of Life that Affect Each Other

If you have already determined your Ascendant sign from page 69, and you have read 'The Meaning of the Zodiac' on page 11, you can apply that knowledge to every area of your life with revealing results. Instead of just looking at yourself, you can see how things like your career and your finances work from the unique point of view of your birth moment.

You will remember how the Ascendant defined which way up the sky was. Once you have it the right way up, then you can divide it into sectors for different areas of life, and see which zodiac signs occupy them. After that, you can interpret each sector of sky in the light of what you know about the zodiac sign which fell in it at the time that you were born.

Below there is a circular diagram of the sky, with the horizon splitting it across the middle. This is the way real horoscopes are usually drawn. In the outer circle, in the space indicated, write the name of your Ascendant sign, not your Sun sign (unless they are the same, of course. If you don't know your time of birth, and so can't work out an Ascendant, use your Sun sign). Make it overlap sectors 12 and 1, so that the degree of your Ascendant within that sign is on the eastern horizon. Now fill in the rest of the zodiac around the circle in sequence, one across each sector boundary. If you've forgotten the sequence, look at the diagram on page 16. When you've done that, draw a symbol for the Sun (☉—a circle with a point at its centre) in one of the sectors which has your Sun sign at its edge. Think about how far through the sign your Sun is; make sure that you have put it in the right sector. Whichever sector this is will be very important to you;

having the Sun there gives a bias to the whole chart, like the weight on one side of a locomotive wheel. You will feel that the activities of that sector (or house, as they are usually called) are most in keeping with your character, and you feel comfortable doing that sort of thing.

Make sure you have got your sums right. As an Arian born in the middle of the afternoon, you might well have Virgo rising, and the Sun in the eighth house, for example.

Now is the time to examine the twelve numbered sections of your own sky, and see what there is to be found.

Angular Houses: 1, 4, 7, 10

These are the houses closest to the horizon and the vertical, reading round in zodiacal sequence. The first house is concerned with you yourself as a physical entity, your appearance, and your health. Most of this has been dealt with in the section on

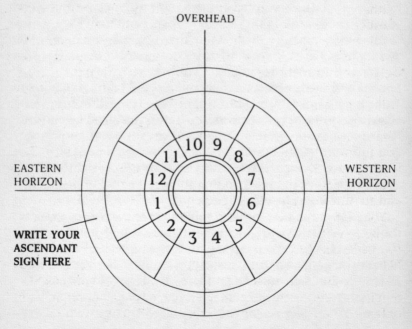

Ascendants. If you have the Sun here, it simply doubles the impact of your Sun sign energies.

Opposite to you is the seventh house, which concerns itself with everybody who is not you. Partners in a business sense, husbands, wives, enemies you are actually aware of (and who therefore stand opposed to you in plain sight) and any other unclassified strangers all belong in the seventh house. You see their motivation as being of the opposite sign to your Ascendant sign, as being something you are not. If you have Capricorn rising, you see them as behaving, and needing to be treated, which is perhaps more accurate, in a Cancerian manner. This is how you approach seventh-house things. Use the keywords from 'The Meaning of the Zodiac' (p. 17) to remind yourself what this is. If you have the Sun in the seventh house you are your own best partner: you may marry late in life, or not at all. Perhaps your marriage will be unsuccessful. It is not a failure; it is simply that you are to a very great extent self-supporting, and have neither the ability nor the need to share yourself completely with another.

The whole business of the first and the seventh is to do with 'me and not-me'. For the personal energies of this relationship to be shown in tangible form, it is necessary to look at the pair of houses whose axis most squarely crosses the first/seventh axis. This is the fourth/tenth. The tenth is your received status in the world, and is the actual answer to the question 'What do you take me for?' No matter what you do, the world will find it best to see you as doing the sort of thing shown by the sign at the start of the tenth house. Eventually, you will start to pursue that kind of activity anyway, because in doing so you get more appreciation and reward from the rest of society.

Your efforts in dealing with others, which is a first/seventh thing, have their result in the tenth, and their origins in the fourth. Expect to find clues there to your family, your home, the beliefs you hold most dear, and the eventual conclusion to your life (not your death, which is a different matter). If you have the Sun in the tenth, you will achieve some measure of prominence or fame; if your Sun is in the fourth, you will do well in property, and your family will be of greater importance to you than is usual.

There is, of course, some give and take between the paired houses. Giving more time to yourself in the first house means that you are denying attention to the seventh, your partner; the reverse also applies. Giving a lot of attention to your career, in the tenth house, stops you from spending quite so much time as you might like with your family or at home. Spending too much time at home means that you are out of the public eye. There is only so much time in a day; what you give to one must be denied to the other.

This cross of four houses defines most people's lives: self, partner, home, and career. An over-emphasis on any of these is to the detriment of the other three, and all the arms of the cross feel and react to any event affecting any single member.

If these four houses have cardinal signs on them in your chart, then you are very much the sort of person who feels that he is in control of his own life, and that it is his duty to shape it into something new, personal, and original. You feel that by making decisive moves with your own circumstances you can actually change the way your life unfolds, and enjoy steering it the way you want it to go.

If these four houses have fixed signs on them in your chart, then you are the sort of person who sees the essential shape of your life as being one of looking after what you were given, continuing in the tradition, and ending up with a profit at the end of it all. Like a farmer, you see yourself as a tenant of the land you inherited, with a responsibility to hand it on in at least as good a condition as it was when you took it over. You are likely to see the main goal in all life's ups and downs as the maintenance of stability and enrichment of what you possess.

If these four houses have mutable signs on them in your chart, then you are much more willing to change yourself to suit circumstances than the other two. Rather than seeing yourself as the captain of your ship, or the trustee of the family firm, you see yourself as free to adapt to challenges as they arise, and if necessary to make fundamental changes in your life, home and career to suit the needs of the moment. You are the sort to welcome change and novelty, and you don't expect to have anything to show for it at the end of the day except experience. There is a strong sense of service in the mutable signs, and if you spend your life working for the welfare of others, then they will have something to show for it while you will not. Not in physical terms, anyway; you will have had your reward by seeing your own energies transformed into their success.

The Succedent Houses: 2, 5, 8, 11

These houses are called succedent because they succeed, or follow on from, the previous four. Where the angular houses define the framework of the life, the succedent ones give substance, and help develop it to its fullest and richest extent, in exactly the same way as fixed signs show the development and maintenance of the elemental energies defined by the cardinal signs.

The second house and the eighth define your resources; how much you have to play with, so to speak. The fifth and eleventh show what you do with it, and how much you achieve. Your immediate environment is the business of the second house. Your tastes in furniture and clothes are here (all part of your immediate environment, if you think about it) as well as your immediate resources, food and cash. Food is a resource because without it you are short of energy, and cash is a resource for obvious reasons. If you have the Sun here you are likely to be fond of spending money, and fond of eating too! You are likely to place value on things that you can buy or possess, and judge your success by your bank balance.

Opposed to it, and therefore dealing with the opposite viewpoint, is the eighth house, where you will find stored money. Savings, bank accounts, mortgages, and all kinds of non-immediate money come under this house. So do major and irreversible changes in your life, because they are the larger environment rather than the immediate one. Surgical operations and death are both in the eighth, because you are not the same person afterwards, and that is an irreversible change. If you have the Sun in the eighth you are likely to be very careful with yourself, and not the sort to expose yourself to any risk; you are also not likely to be short of a few thousand when life gets tight, because eighth house people always have some extra resource tucked away somewhere. You are also likely to benefit from legacies, which are another form of long-term wealth.

To turn all this money into some form of visible wealth you must obviously do something with it, and all forms of self-expression and ambition are found in the fifth and the eleventh houses. The fifth is where you have fun, basically; all that you like to do, all that amuses you, all your hobbies are found there, and a look at the zodiac sign falling in that house in your chart will show you what it is that you like so much. Your children are a fifth-house phenomenon, too; they are an expression of yourself made physical, made from the substance of your body and existence, and given their own. If you have the Sun in the fifth house you are likely to be of a generally happy disposition, confident that life is there to be enjoyed, and sure that something good will turn up.

The eleventh house, in contrast, is not so much what you like doing as what you would like to be doing: it deals with hopes, wishes, and ambitions. It also deals with friends and all social gatherings, because in a similar manner to the first/seventh axis, anybody who is 'not-you' and enjoying themselves must be opposed to you enjoying yourself in the fifth house. If you have the Sun in the eleventh house, you are at your best in a group. You would do well in large organizations, possibly political ones, and will find that you can organize well. You have well-defined ambitions, and know how to realize them, using other people as supporters of your cause.

The oppositions in this cross work just as effectively as the previous set did: cash is either used or stored, and to convert it from one to the other diminishes the first. Similarly, time spent enjoying yourself does nothing for your ambitions and aims, nor does it help you maintain relationships with all the groups of people you know; there again, all work and no play . . .

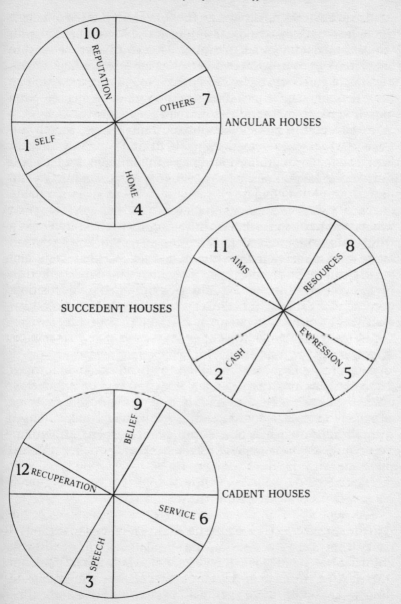

ANGULAR HOUSES

SUCCEDENT HOUSES

CADENT HOUSES

If you have cardinal signs on these four houses in your chart, then you think that using all the resources available to you at any one time is important. Although what you do isn't necessarily important, or even stable, you want to have something to show for it, and enjoying yourself as you go along is important to you. To you, money is for spending, and how your friends see you is possibly more important to you than how you see yourself.

Fixed signs on these four houses will make you reticent, and careful of how you express yourself. You are possibly too busy with the important things of life as you see them, such as your career and long-term prospects, to give much attention to the way you live. You feel it is important to have things of quality, because you have a long-term view of life, and you feel secure when you have some money in the bank, but you don't enjoy your possessions and friends for your own sake. You have them because you feel that you should, not because they are reason enough in themselves.

Mutable signs on these four houses show a flexible attitude to the use of a resource, possibly because the angular houses show that you already have plenty of it, and it is your duty to use it well. You don't mind spending time and money on projects which to you are necessary, and which will have a measurable end result. You see that you need to spend time and effort to bring projects into a completed reality, and you are willing to do that as long as the final product is yours and worth having. You are likely to change your style of living quite frequently during your life, and there may be ambitions which, when fulfilled, fade from your life completely.

The Cadent Houses: 3, 6, 9, 12

The final four houses are called cadent either because they fall away from the angles (horizon and vertical axes), or because they fall towards them, giving their energy towards the formation of the next phase in their existence. Either way, affairs in these houses are nothing like as firm and active as those in the other two sets of four. It may be useful to think of them as being given to mental rather than physical or material activities.

The third and ninth houses are given to thought and speech, with the ninth specializing in incoming thoughts, such as reading, learning and belief (religions of all kinds are ninth-house things), while the third limits itself to speaking and writing, daily chat, and the sort of conversations you have every day. If you have the Sun in the third house, you will be a chatterbox. Talking is something you could do all day, and you love reading. Anything will do—papers, magazines, novels; as long as it has words in it you will like it. You will have the sort of mind that loves accumulating trivia, but you may find that serious study or hard learning is something that you cannot do.

The third house concerns itself with daily conversation, but the ninth is more withdrawn. Study is easy for a ninth-house person, but since all ideal and theoretical thought belongs here, the down-to-earth street-corner reality of the third house doesn't, and so the higher knowledge of the ninth finds no application in daily life. The third-ninth axis is the difference between practical street experience and the refined learning of a university. To give time to one must mean taking time from the other. If you have the Sun in the ninth, you are likely to have a very sure grasp of the theory of things, and could well be an instigator or director of large projects; but you are unable to actually do the things yourself. Knowledge is yours, but application is not.

How this knowledge gets applied in the production of something new is a matter of technique, and technique is the business of the sixth house. The way things get done, both for yourself and for other people's benefit, is all in the sixth. Everything you do on someone else's behalf is there, too. If you have the Sun in the sixth house, you are careful and considerate by nature, much concerned to make the best use of things and to do things in the best way possible. Pride of work and craftsman-ship are guiding words to you; any kind of sloppiness is upsetting. You look after yourself, too; health is a sixth-house thing, and the Sun in the sixth sometimes makes you something of a hypochondriac.

Opposed to the sixth, and therefore opposed to the ideas of doing things for others, mastering the proper technique, and looking after your physical health, is the twelfth house. This is concerned with withdrawing yourself from the world, being on your own, having time to think. Energy is applied to the job in hand in the sixth house, and here it is allowed to grow again without being applied to anything. Recuperation is a good word to remember. All forms of rest are twelfth-house concepts. If you have the Sun in the twelfth house you are an essentially private individual, and there will be times when you need to be on your own to think about things and recover your strength and balance. You will keep your opinions to yourself, and share very little of your emotional troubles with anyone. Yours is most definitely not a life lived out in the open.

These houses live in the shadow of the houses which follow them. Each of them is a preparation for the next phase. If your Sun is in any of these houses, your life is much more one of giving away than of accumulation. You already have the experience and the knowledge, and you will be trying to hand it on before you go, so to speak. Acquisition is something you will never manage on a permanent basis.

If these houses have Cardinal signs on them in your chart, then preparation for things to come is important to you, and you think in straight lines towards a recognized goal. You will have firm and rather simplistic views and beliefs about matters which are not usually described in such terms, such as morality and politics, and you will be used to saying things simply and with meaning. Deception and half-truths, even mild exaggeration, confuse you, because you do not think in that sort of way.

If fixed signs occupy these houses in your horoscope, your thinking is conservative, and your mind, though rich and varied in its imagination, is not truly original. You like to collect ideas from elsewhere and tell yourself that they are your own. You rely on changing circumstances to bring you variety, and your own beliefs and opinions stay fixed to anchor you in a changing world; unfortunately, this can mean a refusal to take in new ideas, shown in your behaviour as a rather appealing old-fashionedness.

Having mutable signs on these houses in your horoscope shows a flexible imagination, though often not a very practical one. Speech and ideas flow freely from you, and you are quick to adapt your ideas to suit the occasion, performing complete changes of viewpoint without effort if required. You seem to have grasped the instinctive truth that mental images and words are not real, and can be changed or erased at will; you are far less inhibited in their use than the other two groups, who regard words as something at least as heavy as cement, and nearly as difficult to dissolve. Periods in the public eye and periods of isolation are of equal value to you; you can use them each for their best purpose, and have no dislike of either. This great flexibility of mind does mean, though, that you lack seriousness of approach at times, and have a happy-go-lucky view of the future, and of things spiritual, which may lead to eventual disappointments and regrets.

Houses are important in a horoscope. The twelve sectors of the sky correspond to the twelve signs of the zodiac, the difference being that the zodiac is a product of the Sun's annual revolution, and the houses are a product (via the Ascendant) of the Earth's daily revolution. They bring the symbolism down one level from the sky to the individual, and they answer the questions which arise when people of the same Sun sign have different lives and different preferences. The house in which the Sun falls, and the qualities of the signs in the houses, show each person's approach to those areas of his life, and the one which will be the most important to him.

Part 4

Aries Trivia

7. Tastes and Preferences

Clothes

Arians are active people, and so have an instinctive dislike of formal clothes; besides, formal clothes usually inhibit rapid movement, and an Arian tries never to allow that to happen. You will be much happier in anything red; it is Mars' colour, and the more you wear of it, the more in tune with yourself you will feel. If you are depressed or out of sorts, and you are not wearing red, then change clothes at once; you will feel much better in your own colour. You don't look too bad in patterns involving straight lines or solid areas of colour, because you match the incisive and bold visual statement thus produced, but you look rather disconcerting in anything with a small or busy pattern, because onlookers see the neatness and fussiness of the small pattern, sense the powerful energies from you, and become confused. You will look good in any kind of sportswear, because the way your planetary energy makes you move your body will always give you an athletic stride; this, when matched to sportswear, gives an overall impression of fitness and readiness for action which suits your character down to the ground. Don't become lazy and wear a tracksuit and trainers the whole time, though; the temptation is enormous, because as an Arian you are lazy about things which don't concern you overmuch, like appearance, and you have a tendency to dress as a child on occasions. Is this because wearing adult clothing suggests a seriousness you try to avoid? Your favourite clothes are probably old ones, and the reasons for this are many. Firstly, they are probably a bit loose, and that helps you move in them. They are comfortable, and that stops you feeling trapped. They served their purpose once, and were fashionable then, so you don't have to think any more about them (the phrase here is likely to be 'I've got a jacket; what do I need another one for?'). Lastly, nobody will complain too much if you go off and do something mildly adventurous in them, so you can get them as dirty as you like. The mind of the child in his muddy jeans who dislikes his restricting Sunday School suit is always there in the Arian, who would rather his clothes allowed for his behaviour than the other way round.

Food and Furnishings

Arians like eating, which is just as well, because they need to if their phenomenal energy output is to be maintained. But notice that they eat because they are hungry, not because they enjoy food as such. Left to themselves, they eat anything which is available at the time, because they don't usually think too hard about what they're going to eat. If you are trying to give a dinner party for an Arian, though, there are one or two preferences you might like to note. Firstly, they usually eat meat. It may be the association with strength and muscle, or it may be the colour (they like red meat). Secondly, they are traditionally supposed to like all sharp, acid, or hot flavours, so a curry will never fail. If you remember the child inside every Arian, and make it easy to eat, your efforts will be appreciated. For a dessert, remember the Arian child again, and serve anything which you know is popular with children.

In their homes, Arians like the furniture plain and strong, perhaps because they tend to bump into it a fair bit. Don't expect fussy furnishings, just solid, much used, much loved pieces which probably don't match, because they were bought individually as the mood took the owner. Ornaments are rare in the Arian environment, because they serve no immediate purpose and the Arian has no sense of nostalgia. The favourite colour will be red again, but there may be some cooler blues to provide contrast. Arians like their music loud, and their toys where they can find and play with them, so the video/stereo systems will be very obvious. Machinery is another Arian pleasure, so the kitchen should be full of tools, especially knives, and there may be machines as ornaments, such as model cars.

Hobbies

Real cars are a source of great joy to Arians, and the quintessential Arian vehicle is the Ferrari. It has every Arian feature: it is bright red (usually), single-minded in its design, highly expressive of its purpose, and blindingly fast. It has no room for any luggage, not much room for any passengers, and is at its best when taking one person a long way at high speed. It is also selfish, self-indulgent, and slightly childish. It is impossible to think of a car which sums up the spirit of Arian energy better. Not every Arian can afford one of course, but wherever possible the Arian will choose the coupé or better still the open-top version of whatever he can afford rather than the saloon, and that rather than the estate. Given a choice of colours he will choose red, and given a choice of engines he will choose the one with either the most power or the most noise. As long as there are sports cars, there will be Arians to buy them, take them to pieces, love them, drive them too fast for their own good, and generally make the rest of us smile indulgently and shake our heads, professing to know better. We are missing out on the pure joy of headlong speed, which is the Arian's birthright.

Other things which Arians enjoy are all mechanized sports, including things like shooting; all combat sports; and all pastimes which include metals or metal tools. This takes some surprising forms—artistic Arians sculpt with metal chisels, or make wrought iron work; musical Arians play in brass bands.

8. Arian Luck

Being lucky isn't a matter of pure luck. It can be engineered. What happens when you are lucky is that a number of correspondences are made between circumstances, people, and even material items, which eventually enable planetary energies to flow quickly and effectively to act with full force in a particular way. If you are part of that chain, or your intentions lie in the same direction as the planetary flow, then you say that things are going your way, or that you are lucky. All you have to do to maximize this tendency is to make sure you are aligned to the flow of energies from the planets whenever you want things to work your way.

It is regular astrological practice to try to reinforce your own position in these things, by attracting energies which are already strongly represented in you. For an Arian, this means Mars, of course, and therefore any 'lucky' number, colour, or whatever for an Arian is simply going to be one which corresponds symbolically to the attributes of Mars.

Mars' colour is red; therefore an Aries person's lucky colour is red, because by wearing it or aligning himself to it, for example by betting on a horse whose jockey's silks are red, or supporting a sporting team whose colours include red, he aligns himself to the energies of Mars, and thereby recharges the Martian energies that are already in him.

An Aries' preferred gemstone is a ruby, because of its colour and the reasons given above. Gemstones are seen as being able to concentrate or focus magical energies, and the colour of the stone shows its correspondence with the energies of a particular planet. Other gemstones are sometimes quoted for Aries, such as the bloodstone or red haematite, but in all cases the colour is the key.

Because Aries is the first sign, your lucky number is 1; all combinations of numbers which add up to 1 by reduction work the same way, so you have a range to choose from. Reducing a number is done by adding its digits until you can go no further. As an example, take 595, $5 + 9 + 5 = 19$, then $1 + 9 = 10$, and finally $1 + 0 = 1$. There you are—595 is a lucky number for you, so to buy a car with those digits in its registration plate would make it a car which, while you had it, you were very fond of, and which served you well.

Mars has its own number, which is 5. The same rules apply as they did with 1. Mars also has its own day, Tuesday (mardi in French, which means Mars' day), and Aries has both a time with which it is associated (sunrise), and a direction (the East). If you have something important to do, and you manage to put it into action early in the morning of Tuesday 5 January (month number 1, remember), then you will have made sure that you will get the result best suited to you, by aligning yourself to your own planet and helping its energies flow through you and your activity unimpeded.

Mars also has a metal associated with it, and in the Middle Ages people wore jewellery made of their planetary metals for luck, or self-alignment and emphasis, whichever way you want to describe it. In the case of Aries and Mars, that metal is iron, which is a pity in some ways, because personal ornaments made of iron have never been as popular as silver and gold. Perhaps this is why Arians get such great pleasure from their cars, which are, after all, personal tokens made of iron and steel.

There are plants and herbs for each planet, and foods too. Among the more edible plants are basil, coriander, garlic, ginger – and tobacco.

There is almost no end to the list of correspondences between the planets and everyday items, and many more can be made if you have a good imagination. They are lucky for Arians if you know what makes them so, and if you believe them to be so; the essence of the process lies in linking yourself and the object of your intent with some identifiable token of your own planet, such as its colour or number, and strengthening yourself thereby. The stronger you are, then the more frequently you will be able to achieve the result you want—and that's all that luck is, isn't it?

A Final Word

By the time you reach here, you will have learnt a great deal more about yourself. At least, I hope you have.

You will probably have noticed that I appear to have contradicted myself in some parts of the book, and repeated myself in others, and there are reasons for this. It is quite likely that I have said that your Sun position makes you one way, while your Ascendant makes you the opposite. There is nothing strange about this; nobody is consistent, the same the whole way through—everybody has contradictory sides to their character, and knowing some more about your Sun sign and your Ascendant will help you to label and define those contradictory elements. It won't do anything about dealing with them, though—that's your job, and always has been. The only person who can live your horoscope is you. Astrology won't make your problems disappear, and it never has been able to; it simply defines the problems more clearly, and enables you to look for answers.

Where I have repeated myself it is either to make the point for the benefit of the person who is only going to read that section of the book, or because you have a double helping of the energy of your sign, as in the instance of the Sun and Ascendant in the same sign.

I hope you found the relationships section useful; you may well find that the Sun-to-Ascendant comparison is just as useful in showing you how you fit in with your partner as the usual Sun-to-Sun practice.

Where do you go from here? If you want to learn more about astrology, and see how all of the planets fit into the picture of the sky as it was at your birth, then you must either consult an astrologer or learn how to do it for yourself. There is quite a lot of astrology around these days; evening classes are not too hard to find and there are groups of enthusiasts up and down the country. There are also plenty of books which will show you how to draw up and interpret your own horoscope.

One thing about doing it yourself, which is an annoyance unless you are aware of it in advance: to calculate your horoscope properly you will need to know where the planets were in the sky when you were born, and you usually have to buy this data separately in a book called an ephemeris. The reason that astrology books don't have this data in them is that to include enough for everybody who is likely to buy the book would make the book as big as a phone directory, and look like a giant book of log tables, which is a bit off-putting. You can buy ephemerides (the plural) for any single year, such as the one of your birth. You can also buy omnibus versions for the whole century.

So, you will need two books, not one: an ephemeris, and a book to help you draw up and interpret your horoscope. It's much less annoying when you *know* you're going to need two books.

After that, there are lots of books on the more advanced techniques in the Astrology Handbook series, also from the Aquarian Press. Good though the books are, there is no substitute for being taught by an astrologer, and no substitute at all for practice. What we are trying to do here is provide a vocabulary of symbols taken from the sky so that you and your imagination can make sense of the world you live in; the essential element is your imagination, and you provide that.

Astrology works perfectly well at Sun sign level, and it works perfectly well at deeper levels as well; you can do it with what you want. I hope that, whatever you do with it, it is both instructive and satisfying to you—and fun, too.

RELATING

Liz Greene Since it was first published in 1977 this book has become a classic of modern astrological literature. It is now reprinted with a new introduction by Liz Greene. Her insights are as fresh and exciting as ever and the ideas she explores about the nature of relating have increased relevance today.

She shows how to use basic astrological concepts symbolically and practically, in a framework of Jungian psychology, to illuminate the ways in which people relate to each other on both conscious and unconscious levels.

RELATING remains a key text for any reader interested in the psychological dimensions of astrology; but it is also a book for anyone who wants to know more about themselves and the way they relate to others.

'If you only read one astrology book this year, make it Liz Greene's *Relating* . . . Even if you plan to read only one book of any kind this year, *Relating* would still be an excellent choice.' — *Horoscope Magazine*

'A thoughtful and scholarly book which marries the profundities of Jungian psychology with the age-old science of astrology to provide fresh insights into ourselves and our relationships.' — *Psychology Today*

'A remarkably good book and highly recommended . . . this book deserves to be on every astrologer's shelf, if not on the shelf of anyone who cares about his or her relationships with others.' — *Prediction*

ASTRO-PICK YOUR PERFECT PARTNER

M. E. Coleman *What makes you fall in love and out of it? How can you tell the difference between sexual attractions and long-term caring? Does loving someone mean you can overcome incompatibility of life styles and upbringing? Can you handle lifetime commitment or can't you?* Today, these are the questions that everyone worries and wonders about as drastic social changes alter the meaning of marriage, morals, and even the definition of love itself. This book can help you find the answers to all your relationship problems. Written by a university-qualified psychologist, it shows you how to assess accurately and quickly your own special needs in love and sex, then how to rate their compatibility with those of your existing or intended partner. The technique is called astro-analysis because it merges the interpretation of personality traits shown in the horoscope chart with modern methods of psychological analysis. As you work with it, you'll discover facets and drives in your own nature you didn't know existed. You'll see those you care most about in a new and revealing light. Easy-to-use Compatibility Rating Tables ensure you make no mistakes and come up with right answers every time!

SUNS AND LOVERS

The Astrology of Sexual Relationships

Penny Thornton. It doesn't seem to matter how experienced – or inexperienced – you are, when it comes to love and romance there just *isn't* a fool proof formula. . . but this book does its best to provide one! THE definitive astrological guide to sexual relationships, this book is based upon the accumulated wisdom, and observations of centuries of dedicated astrologists. Reveals:

- In-depth analysis of astrological types
- Male and female profiles for each star sign
- Zodiacal attitudes to intimate relationships
- Most compatible – and incompatible – partners

Each general star sign analysis is concluded with amazingly frank reflections, often based upon personal interviews, with many famous personalities including: Bob Champion; Suzi Quatro; Colin Wilson; Jeremy Irons; HRH The Princess Anne; HRH The Duke of York; Martin Shaw; Barbara Cartland; Twiggy and many more. Written in an easy-to-read style, and packed with illuminating and fascinating tit-bits, this book is compulsive reading for anyone likely to have *any sort* of encounter with the opposite sex!

HOW TO ASTRO-ANALYSE YOURSELF AND OTHERS.

Mary Coleman. Easy to follow, step-by-step instructions on the art of astro-analysis a blend of traditional astrology and modern psychology that provides practical solutions to the conundrums of life, love and sex.

- Discover why you do the things you do.
- Plan your life instead of just 'letting it happen'.
- Make the most of yourself and your relationships.

Master the technique of astro-anaysis and discover a more confident 'you' emerging, and the path to a happier, more satisying future opening out before you. The day you read this book could be the first day of the rest of your life.

THE ASTROLOGY WORKBOOK

This book is YOUR introduction to FUN, FORTUNE and FASCINATION

Cordelia Mansall, in clear and easy-to-understand language, demystifies the ancient science of astrology and shows how YOU can profit from this exact, and increasingly respected, wisdom.

Discover

- When to expect your 'vitality surges'
- The crisis ages of your life
- Your hidden talents
- The latent potentialities of your children

The whole of our lives are shaped by cosmic forces. Astrology is the study of these forces and their effects upon our lives *both now and in the future*. The author shows how it can be used to bring a deeper understanding to the problems encountered in personal relationships, indicate the most favourable times for major life-style changes and present an important balance between science and spirituality. *Discover your place in the overall scheme of the universe with* THE ASTROLOGY WORKBOOK by **Cordelia Mansall D. F. Astrol. S.**